Praise for *Safe and*

"Professionals seeking viable alternatives to the disrespect and bullying ... he school environment can immediately employ the step-by-step strategies nested within a robust and coherent framework"

—Gerald Monk, Professor, San Diego State University
Co-author with John Winslade of *Narrative Mediation*
and *Narrative Counseling in Schools*

"This book's restorative justice approach is unique and powerful, offering students an opportunity to process resolutions in an inclusive rather than isolating environment."

—Trish Hatch, Associate Professor and Director,
School Counseling Program, San Diego State University
Co-author, ASCA National Model

"This book is a welcome alternative to the blunt-weapon option of "zero tolerance," offering a goldmine of material that is both informed by research and illustrated through accessible real-life case vignettes."

—David Paré, Faculty of Education, University of Ottawa. Director of
The Glebe Institute, A Centre for Constructive and Collaborative Practice

"The authors take one of the most elegant, touching, and successful approaches I have seen to what many regard as an intractable problem. I can assure you that 'Undercover Anti-Bullying Teams' is worth the price of the book alone."

—David Epston, Co-author of *Narrative Means to
Therapeutic Ends and Playful Approaches to
Serious Problems: Narrative Therapy With Children and Their Families*

"The most comprehensive non-punitive approach to school conflict resolution in one book! As both a school social worker and narrative therapist, I am appreciative to John Winslade and Michael Williams for this solid practice-based book that will be applicable to and inspiring for anyone who works in schools."

—Angel Yuen, School Social Worker
Toronto District School Board

"Some might object that it is not the role of schools to teach conflict resolution. However, 21st century learners will work in a world that requires global cooperation in collaborative work settings, and how else will they learn to recognize the complexity of every situation and community? I recommend this text for school administrators, counselors, and those seeking to help build relationships that are peaceful and just, and which restore humanity and honor to all."

—Jay Fiene, Dean, College of Education,
California State University San Bernardino

Safe and Peaceful
SCHOOLS

Addressing
Conflict
and
Eliminating
Violence

JOHN WINSLADE
MICHAEL WILLIAMS

CORWIN
A SAGE Company

CORWIN
A SAGE Company

FOR INFORMATION:

Corwin
A SAGE Publications Company
2455 Teller Road
Thousand Oaks, California 91320
(800) 233-9936
Fax: (800) 417-2466
www.corwinpress.com

SAGE Publications Ltd.
1 Oliver's Yard
55 City Road
London EC1Y 1SP
United Kingdom

SAGE Publications India Pvt. Ltd.
B 1/I 1 Mohan Cooperative Industrial Area
Mathura Road, New Delhi 110 044
India

SAGE Publications Asia-Pacific Pte. Ltd.
33 Pekin Street #02-01
Far East Square
Singapore 048763

Acquisitions Editor: Jessica Allan
Associate Editor: Allison Scott
Editorial Assistant: Lisa Whitney
Production Editor: Libby Larson
Copy Editor: Teresa Herlinger
Typesetter: C&M Digitals (P) Ltd.
Proofreader: Theresa Kay
Indexer: Diggs Publication Services
Cover Designer: Michael Dubowe
Permissions Editor: Karen Ehrmann

Copyright © 2012 by Corwin

All rights reserved. When forms and sample documents are included, their use is authorized only by educators, local school sites, and/or noncommercial or nonprofit entities who have purchased the book. Except for that usage, no part of this book may be reproduced or utilized in any form or by any means, electronic or mechanical, including photocopying, recording, or by any information storage and retrieval system, without permission in writing from the publisher.

Printed in the United States of America

Library of Congress Cataloging-in-Publication Data

Winslade, John.

Safe and peaceful schools : addressing conflict and eliminating violence / John Winslade, Michael Williams.

p. cm.
Includes bibliographical references and index.

ISBN 978-1-4129-8675-5 (pbk.)

1. School violence—United States—Prevention.
2. Schools—United States—Safety measures.
3. Conflict management—Study and teaching—United States.

I. Williams, Michael. II. Title.

LB3013.3.W556 2012
371.7'820973—dc23   2011039020

SUSTAINABLE FORESTRY INITIATIVE

Certified Chain of Custody
Promoting Sustainable Forestry
www.sfiprogram.org
SFI-01268

SFI label applies to text stock

This book is printed on acid-free paper

11 12 13 14 15 10 9 8 7 6 5 4 3 2 1

Contents

Preface

PURPOSE OF THIS BOOK

This book arose out of our mutual interest in specific approaches to conflict resolution in schools. We have both worked at mediation, facilitated restorative conferences, and offered counseling and conflict coaching to individuals. We have developed undercover anti-bullying teams and led groups dedicated to eliminating violence. But all of this work has never, to our knowledge, been brought together in a comprehensive systematic program.

What would a school look like if it were to say to itself, "We are going to manage the conflicts that happen in our school in a respectful way that addresses problems, reduces violence, restores harm when it occurs, and produces a climate of inclusion, without relying on heavy punishments"? We were interested in what kinds of processes would be needed to make relationships between people in a school community a deliberate focus of attention.

We also had a perspective on conflict resolution in mind that we wanted to elaborate. It grows out of what began as "narrative mediation" (Winslade & Monk, 2000, 2008) but has since transformed into a variety of forms of conflict resolution that have stretched way beyond the parameters of what might be called mediation. It draws from a robust set of ideas known in different places as poststructuralism, social constructionism, and postmodernism, although we would caution that we do not endorse every expression of these concepts. The practices of narrative therapy and community work are present in a range of practices represented in this book. We have never before brought all of these practices together in one place. This book is an attempt to do so.

We want to address the needs of school leaders who are interested in designing a school climate in which conflict is effectively managed. By "managed," we mean addressed and handled in ways that are respectful of all involved, rather than controlled from above. And we also envisage an audience of school counselors and psychologists who are intimately involved in implementing many of the strategies outlined in the book. The dual professional audience reflects a conviction about the need for partnership between policy and practice, between designing programs and implementing them. In this book, we often take readers into the micro-practice of detailed conversations. We realize that this detail will not always be necessary for school leaders to master, but we want them to understand how these practices work in order to be able to support the school counselors and psychologists who will implement them. We also want the same school counselors and psychologists to play a role in the design and construction of systems of conflict management in a school, rather than leave all such decision making and policy design to school leaders. In the United States, we believe that the ASCA National Model for school counseling and the trend toward "response to intervention" (RTI) modes of practice fit well with the comprehensive approach we are outlining here.

We often refer to the school counselor as the skilled practitioner who will implement these practices. Some school counselors, however, have the expertise to do this work but may choose not to. Often it might be a school psychologist, sometimes a school social worker, and sometimes a youth worker who implements the practices. There are also many teachers who are interested in and capable of taking up some of the practices outlined in this book. In different places, there are various designations of professional roles that can be involved. In the United States, there are "student management specialists," for example. In New Zealand, there are "resource teachers of learning and behavior." In parts of Europe, there are "pedagogs." We are not picky about "who does what." We have put these ideas together in a comprehensive and theoretically consistent way to encourage school administrators and educational professionals to try something different.

We often hear that school counselors are just involved in class scheduling and are not trained to do real counseling or conflict resolution work. We feel this is an excuse for poor standards of professional work. Our intention is to provide tools to those who aim for high standards of professional practice. School leaders should expect no less from their school counselors.

There is compelling research support for the efficacy of restorative practices in schools, for mediation practice in general across a variety of settings (including schools), for anger management groups, for undercover anti-bullying teams, and for counseling. But the idea of bringing all these ideas together into a program is still in its infancy, and we are looking for opportunities to work with schools willing to implement them in a serious way. Research confirmation of the worthiness of doing so must follow the further development in practice of these ideas rather than lead it. This is a book about practice.

BACKGROUND TO WRITING THE BOOK

The authors first met when Mike was studying for a Master of Education degree at the University of Waikato (New Zealand) and John was a member of the teaching faculty. John supervised Mike's final dissertation and encouraged him to continue to apply narrative ideas in his work as a school counselor. By chance, it happened that Mike was working at the same school where 10 years earlier John had also been a school counselor.

Mike renewed contact with John as he began to develop the undercover teams approach in his work with bullying. Together they started to articulate this work through writing several articles about it. Conversations and writing efforts began to include a focus on mediation as well, and gradually the idea of writing a book that advocated for a comprehensive program started to emerge. The book has gradually taken shape through many e-mail exchanges, occasional phone or Skype calls, and annual meetings in New Zealand.

Since 2003, John has been based in California but still makes regular visits back to New Zealand and also to Edgewater College, where Mike still works. At California State University, San Bernardino, John has taught school counseling and has developed a sharper feel for how these practices can take shape in an American context.

The writing of this book is based on a partnership across two countries: New Zealand and the United States. It is also intentionally a partnership between authors who work, respectively, in a high school and a university. The stories of practice that populate and enliven this book nearly all come from Mike's work in a New Zealand high school. There is consequently a New Zealand flavor to many of these stories and a high school bias. We have tried to explain these in a way that will make sense to practitioners in other contexts, but there will still be some work that readers have to do to translate them into their own world.

There are many places in the United States and in other countries where restorative practices are being developed, and there are schools in the United States that are experimenting with undercover anti-bullying teams. Michelle Myers, in San Bernardino, for example, has been successfully implementing this approach in an elementary school. There is a substantial literature on anger management groups, too, but they have seldom been written about from the perspective represented in this book.

WHAT TO EXPECT IN EACH CHAPTER

The first two chapters of this book are designed to set the scene. The first one addresses the nature of conflict and points out how serious the problem of violence in schools really is. It also cites a major review of the well-known policy of "zero tolerance" for violence and shows how its outcomes are not as compelling as its image. We argue that another approach is needed and start to articulate what that approach might look like. We also relate the principles on which our approach is based to the need to prepare young people to become democratic citizens.

Chapter 2 sets out the perspective from which the book is written. It outlines what is distinctive about a narrative approach to conflict resolution and introduces many of the concepts that will be put to specific use in later chapters.

Chapter 3 focuses on the use of counseling in situations where conflict is happening or has happened. Individual conflict coaching from a relational perspective is outlined. There is a section on deconstructing rules with students. Then we deal with those occasions where conflict has led to a traumatic event and counseling needs to be about "postvention" rather than prevention or intervention. Principles and practices for counseling individuals and groups in relation to trauma are outlined and explained.

Chapters 4 and 5 are about mediation. In Chapter 4, we outline and illustrate a narrative process of mediation by a school counselor. In Chapter 5, we discuss the development of peer mediation programs in schools. We include a list of issues for schools to resolve in the establishment of a peer mediation program and outline an initial training program for peer mediators.

Chapters 6 and 7 are about restorative practices in schools. Chapter 6 outlines and illustrates a restorative conferencing process to be used to address serious disciplinary offenses. Chapter 7 expands from the full-scale conference to outline restorative conversations of various levels of intensity.

Chapter 8 takes us into the classroom for the purposes of a circle conversation. It sketches some of the histories of circle conversations and shows how they can be used to addresses conflicts that have surfaced in the set of relationships in a class, rather than in any particular pair of students.

Chapter 9 targets the relational narratives around bullying and relational aggression. It shows how the bullying relationship can be transformed by the use of undercover anti-bullying teams.

In Chapter 10, we focus on the use of classroom guidance lessons to address social issues that can be the basis of conflict within the school. These lessons are designed to engage students to think about differences between people in ways that reduce violence and destructive conflict.

Chapter 11 is about group counseling. It is about helping some students who are caught up in patterns of violent behavior or loss of temper to make personal changes that will reduce the likelihood of them hurting other people. We have eschewed the usual title of anger management groups and called them "facing up to violence" groups. The chapter explains why.

In Chapter 12, the threads that run through the previous chapters are tied together. We outline a list of critical questions to be used by school leaders in deciding which of the approaches previously outlined should be implemented. We also address training needs that these methods require.

ACKNOWLEDGMENTS

There are many people who deserve our acknowledgment and gratitude for their contribution to the development of this project. We would like to acknowledge the students and teachers at Edgewater College, because without them this work would never have been written. It is the rich environment of the school that has provided the stories in this book. All are real-life accounts of the struggles that some young people face and overcome. Only the names have been changed. They have been the source and inspiration for the examples of mediation and peer mediation, circle conversations, restorative conferences, and undercover teams. The school principal, Allan Vester, and the Board of Trustees have encouraged Mike to present these findings in many forums.

Gerald Monk has been John's close colleague for many years in the development of narrative practice in conflict resolution. He has read a draft of this book and has offered encouragement and support, and he is implementing many of these ideas in a project in San Diego.

Wendy Drewery and the Restorative Practices Development Team at the University of Waikato in New Zealand also deserve acknowledgment. At various times, this team has included Angus MacFarlane, Maria Kecskemeti, Kathy Cronin-Lampe, Ron Cronin-Lampe, Donald McMenamin, Helen Adams, and Kerry Jenner. Their work is present in the spirit of many of the processes we have written about.

It was Bill Hubbard who first introduced Mike in 2004 to the idea of undercover teams and coined the term. Bill Hubbard also provided Mike with much of the inspiration for using circle conversations in the classroom. He has also been a pioneer of restorative practices in a number of New Zealand high schools. In his development of undercover teams, Bill drew especially on the "no blame" approach developed originally by Maines and Robinson in the United Kingdom. The translation of this work into a mode that is informed by the narrative metaphor is something that Mike and John are responsible for, but we are grateful for the groundbreaking work that Bill Hubbard did.

Mike would also like to acknowledge the personal support from his friend Roger Moltzen who has offered consistent encouragement for the development of Mike's work in schools and for his articulation of it in writing. Mike's wife, Jennie, also deserves appreciation. She listens to him and asks the questions that lie beyond the understanding of those who are new to this work.

John's wife, Lorraine, has also contributed to the writing of this book through many moments of conversation and constant encouragement. He is happy to be able to honor her support in print.

The students and faculty in the counseling programs at California State University, San Bernardino, and at the University of Waikato also deserve a mention. Students have provided an audience for John to test out his explanations for these ideas and have asked the questions that help make them relevant to various contexts of practice.

We also appreciate the efforts of all at Corwin. Acquisitions editor Jessica Allan first saw possibility in the proposal for this book. Teresa Herlinger has provided helpful copyediting. And the eight reviewers, whose comments helped us a great deal, are all owed a debt of gratitude. Their suggestions, comments, and criticisms all helped improve the book.

Last but not least, we extend our appreciation to our readers. Long before you ever knew it, you were present in our writing as we sought to anticipate your needs, concerns, and responses. You have guided our writing more than you know and long before we were able to guide your reading.

Corwin would also like to acknowledge the following reviewers:

Scott Hollinger
Instructional Coach
Former High School Principal
Communities
Foundation of Texas
Dallas, TX

Neil MacNeill
Principal
Ellenbrook Primary School
Ellenbrook, Australia

Amanda Mayeaux
School Improvement Coordinator
Ascension Parish Schools
Geismar, LA

Katy Olweiler
Counselor
Lakeside School
Seattle, WA

Joyce Stout
Elementary School Counselor
Redondo Beach Unified School District
Torrance, CA

Brigitte Tennis
Founder, Headmistress, and eighth-grade teacher
Stella Schola Middle School in Lake Washington School District
Redmond, WA

1

Understanding Conflict in Schools

CONFLICT IS NORMAL

Conflict is ordinary. That is the first thing that needs to be acknowledged. Even in the most homogeneous of schools, differences among students and teachers are always so nuanced that conflict is inevitable. In the pursuit of various agendas, people always bump into other people's agendas.

Schools are a microcosm of the rest of society. Gather together a group of adults and ask them whether they have ever experienced conflict, and you will meet with laughter. Of course they have. Everyone has. As generalizations go, this is a safe one to make.

Conflict is inevitable. It results from the interplay of differences between people. Since people differ in many ways, in their cultural backgrounds and assumptions, their personal styles, their worldviews and perspectives, and their hopes and aspirations, there will frequently be places where they rub against each other. This is as true in school communities as in other places in the social world. Schools do not need to aim for an environment in which conflict is never manifest, so much as an environment in which conflict is handled and managed effectively, so that differences are respected, competing cultural perspectives are valued, and individual students and teachers are heard and included in the conversation—all so that educational activity can proceed.

On the other hand, ask people what it is like to experience conflict, and you will hear how often conflict does not go well. People get hurt by it. It is often managed poorly. Constructive ways of moving forward are frequently not found. Rifts occur and pain is produced. Much energy is expended thinking about conflict, which could be harnessed for other purposes. Sometimes conflict generates violence, and the hurt is magnified tenfold.

Actually, handling conflict constructively is challenging. We learn how to do it in our families and schools often haphazardly. There is seldom a systematic curriculum for learning to get on with others and resolve differences. Students, therefore, do not always learn how to handle conflict. They are sometimes lectured and advised to do it better but often without being shown or given the chance to practice the specific skills of doing so.

In this book, we aim to offer a range of strategies that together amount to a comprehensive program for addressing various types of conflict in a school community. It is not sufficient to introduce a single intervention, such as a peer mediation program, and expect it to deal with everything. In the application of these strategies, we hope that both students and teachers can learn to coexist peacefully and that they can, therefore, get on with the job of teaching and learning.

From time to time, it is inevitable that there should be tension and sometimes conflict among educators, between schools and their communities, between individual students and among groups of students, between students and teachers, and between administrators and teachers. What is needed is an explicit recognition that this is all normal and that the school is prepared to handle it. Handling it involves establishing procedures for people to assert different perspectives; influence each other; listen; and reach resolutions that incorporate multiple perspectives, rather than imposing singular ones. Effective leadership does not require the ability to always know what the best decisions are, so much as attention to the design of processes for constructively handling differences and, sometimes, outbreaks of conflict.

VIOLENCE IS A PROBLEM

If conflict needs to be normalized and learning how to address it made into a priority, that does not mean that we should accept the inevitability of violence. Violence is a problem in schools.

We do not need a library full of rocket science to appreciate that children who are afraid of being hurt, or are upset and angry, are in no state of mind to learn things. Effective learning takes place in a context of emotional calmness and enjoyment, not one dominated by anxiety, anger, or fear. Nel Noddings (2002) is a leading educational thinker who has stated it clearly:

> Through more than five decades of teaching and mothering, I have noticed also that children (and adults too) learn best when they are happy. (p. 2)

Noddings (2002) suggests that it is not just the occurrence of violence but also the threat of it, the fear of it, or the witnessing of it happening to others that affects the ability to learn. Just how bad a problem violence in schools is was put into perspective by a review released by United States Attorney General Eric Holder in October 2009. Announcing the publication of this review in Chicago, where concern about youth violence has become concentrated, Holder said,

> The Department of Justice is releasing a new study today that measures the effects of youth violence in America, and the results are staggering. More than 60 percent of the children surveyed were exposed to violence in the past year, either directly or indirectly. Nearly half of children and adolescents were assaulted at least once, and more than one in ten were injured as a result. Nearly one-quarter were the victim of a robbery, vandalism or theft, and one in sixteen were victimized sexually. Those numbers are astonishing, and they are unacceptable. We simply cannot stand for an epidemic of violence that robs our youth of their childhood and perpetuates a cycle in which today's victims become tomorrow's criminals. (n.p.)

The National Survey of Children's Exposure to Violence (Slowikowski, 2009) found that 46.3% of children had been assaulted at least once in the previous year, including 14.9% who were assaulted with a weapon. Of these, 10% were injured in the assault. Meanwhile, 6.1% were victims of sexual violation, 9.8% had witnessed family violence, 13% were victims of bullying within the last year, and 21.6% during their lifetimes. Other data (U.S. Department of Education, Institute of Education Sciences, 2007) suggest a higher figure for victims of bullying between the ages of 12 and 18: 32% in the previous year, of whom 4% were subject to electronic bullying (via the Internet, or text messaging).

To keep these figures in perspective, the majority of children are still not directly exposed to violence, nor does the evidence support a growing sense of alarm about a worsening situation. The American Psychological Association (APA) Zero Tolerance Task Force (2008) reported that

> the evidence does not support an assumption that violence in schools is out of control. Serious and deadly violence remain a relatively small proportion of school disruptions, and the data have consistently indicated that school violence and disruption have remained stable, or even decreased somewhat, since approximately 1985. (p. 855)

For those who are exposed to violence, however, the data still point to the potential seriousness of the problem of violence in the lives of children. We say "potential" seriousness out of respect for the many young people who are resilient in the face of violence. They do not accept violence as normal or as an ordinary aspect of life. It is not automatic for exposure to violence to lead to psychological harm, but there is a clear enough risk that the traumatic effects of violence on children have to be taken seriously.

For those growing up in poverty, the situation is of heightened concern. A recent study (Kracke & Hahn, 2008) noted that 43% of low-income African American children had witnessed a murder and 56% had witnessed a stabbing, while comparable figures for upper-middle-class youth were 1% and 9%, respectively. A moment's thought suggests that for these children, learning and performance on tests are going to be affected and that simplistic measures to "close the gaps" in learning outcomes are not going to succeed without addressing the effects of violence.

We could go a lot further in detailing the problems of violence, but that is not the purpose of this book. Spreading alarm about problems by citing statistics does not in itself change anything. It may indeed whip up fear or anger and unleash responses that are less than effective. It is more important to offer a range of practical ideas that might help address the problem. That is the aim of this book.

ZERO TOLERANCE DOES NOT WORK

First, however, let us note some common solutions that have been tried. On principle, if current solutions are not working as we would wish, we should try something different. Many school leaders and administrators have moved to get tough and take strong action against violence. Since the 1990s, a wave of schools and school districts have instituted "zero tolerance" policies for violent behavior. Originally devised for the enforcement of laws against drug trafficking, the concept of zero tolerance was adapted for use against violent behavior, especially after some high-profile school shooting incidents in the 1990s. While there is considerable variation in how such policies are interpreted, these policies usually mandate

> the application of predetermined consequences, most often severe and punitive in nature, that are intended to be applied regardless of the seriousness of behavior, mitigating circumstances, or situational context. (APA Zero Tolerance Task Force, 2008, p. 852)

Most often, the predetermined consequences involve removal of the offender from the school, on the assumption that the relational climate in the school for other students will be improved and that future offenders will be deterred. The perpetrators of violent behavior are identified and zero tolerance is extended to these persons, rather than to violent behaviors. They are suspended or expelled from school. The implication is that violent practices are natural features of the personhood of some individuals and that the school community should not extend any tolerance to those individuals. We would call this an action based on an *essentialist* assumption. It assumes that violence is part of the "essence" of the personhood of the perpetrator of violence. The result often has been that those who practice violence are themselves subjected to the symbolic violence (Bourdieu & Passeron, 1977) of the school authorities and are thrown out of school.

There is one big problem with this approach: It does not work. That is, it does not work if we take as our goal the reduction of violence in schools and increasing a sense of safety for students. The American Psychological Association–commissioned task force, noted above, was formed to investigate the effects of zero tolerance policies in schools. The report by this task force (2008) argued strongly against the effectiveness and value of zero tolerance policies in schools. They concluded bluntly, "Zero tolerance has not been shown to improve school climate or school safety" (p. 860). The evidence "consistently flies in the face of . . . [the] beliefs" (p. 860) that removing disruptive students from school will improve the school experience for others. Instead, zero tolerance is actually shown to effectively *increase* disruptive behavior and dropout rates and to lead to higher rates of misbehavior among those who are suspended. Schools with higher rates of suspension also do not show higher rates of academic performance, even when socioeconomic differences are taken into account.

Zero tolerance approaches may satisfy the righteous urge to act decisively and punitively, but they do not appear to teach young people to resolve conflict or to eschew violence. One example of the ridiculous responses to which a zero tolerance policy can lead occurred in an Arizona elementary school. A 6-year-old boy one day brought a toy gun to school and pointed it at another child and talked about killing him. Rigid adherence to a zero tolerance policy meant that this boy was escorted off the school property and taken away in a police car! The official response was way over the top of what would be indicated by discretion and wisdom.

Zero tolerance policies do not even succeed at scaring young people into behaving more prosocially. As the APA report suggests, young people often do things that violate other people on the basis of immaturity or as a result of not yet having learned to think through particular consequences. To consign them to the prison pipeline (which is often what happens when students are sent off to juvenile detention) ignores the developmental dimension that should always be considered when young people offend.

A COMPREHENSIVE APPROACH

What is needed is a fresh approach. While no approach can provide all the answers, in this book we are seeking to offer a fresh perspective. It is based on a particular philosophy of narrative practice, which we shall outline in more detail in Chapter 2. There have been publications that have promised much in the way of reduction of violence on the basis of a single intervention. Zero tolerance policies are often used like this, for example. They may even prove to be more effective if used in combination with a range of other approaches but, on current evidence, they are less than effective on their own. Some have advocated peer mediation programs and we have seen examples of such programs doing wonderful work but they cannot address all problems of violence on their own. In some parts of the world such as New Zealand, where both authors of this book have worked as school counselors, such counselors were originally introduced into schools expressly to reduce "juvenile delinquency" (Besley, 2002). But counseling on its own makes little impact on the overall pattern of school violence. In other instances, programs to reduce bullying have been instituted. But not all violence fits within the standard definition of bullying.

What is needed for a school to become serious about creating a climate that is free of violence and where conflict is handled constructively is to use a comprehensive range of approaches on the basis of thoughtful decision making about what is most appropriate in a particular situation. There is no magic silver bullet that will transform a school climate with one intervention. Zero tolerance is no silver bullet. Neither is peer mediation. Neither is the teaching of relationship skills. We advocate having a range of approaches, from which the most appropriate response needs to be selected for each situation.

Sometimes what is needed may be mediation, sometimes counseling. On other occasions, a restorative conference or mini-conference may be called for, and on others, referral to a "facing up to violence" group. We shall introduce a range of these practices here and advocate for a comprehensive package approach. We shall also include targeted classroom guidance lessons aimed at reducing interactions that lead to violence. In addition, we shall outline an approach to instances of bullying that is proving very effective in circumstances where it has been tried. It is called the undercover anti-bullying team.

We are conscious of especially addressing school administrators, on the one hand, and school counselors and school psychologists on the other. Both groups need to work together for these approaches to work. School counselors and psychologists bring the professional expertise for these approaches to be carried out, and school leaders and administrators need to be involved in the decision making that implements the approach of choice in any single instance.

Before describing the range of approaches to address violence, we want to think further about some basic assumptions that will guide the work outlined in this book. We are taking a philosophical position here. Not everyone would agree with us. One of the difficulties of working against violence in schools is that assumptions are often not shared. We would only suggest that you consider trying out some of these ideas as working assumptions simply because they are different. They therefore have a chance of being fresh and not being just "more of the same that we have already tried."

WHAT IS VIOLENCE?

The question, "What is violence?" sounds so obvious as to be redundant, but answering it is not as simple as it sounds. Most people are fairly sure they can recognize violence when they see it, and there are many actions that nearly everyone would agree can be called violent. But there is always an interpretive element to the description of violence, and it sometimes includes an interpretation of degrees of seriousness, or includes a calculation in which some violence is considered justifiable and some not.

What teachers especially have in their minds to define violence leads to paying attention to certain practices and not others, or to certain students and not others. Therefore, it is important for a school staff to define the kinds of actions they will work to address and change.

The definition of violence that most people hold is that it involves the exercise of too much force. This interpretation focuses on an implicit calculation of the amount of aggression used. A certain degree of force is considered tolerable, or excusable in certain contexts. But an action is violent if it uses too much physical force, especially if it results in physical harm to another.

A more useful definition of violence focuses on the *process of violation*, on what gets violated. From this perspective, some actions violate people's rights, especially their right to act on their own behalf, to defend themselves, to express their own thoughts, and to do things for themselves and others.

Brenda Solomon (2006) raises this distinction. Solomon is particularly interested in what young people learn in school about violence, and she researched what was called violence in the interpretation of teachers. She found that a considerable amount of physical force used by students in school against other students is not called violent because it does not cross the threshold of "too much force." Such interpretations mostly focus on boys' play. When teachers made comments about how "kids" behave, they were usually talking about how boys behave. When they talked about girls, or gay or lesbian students, or racial minorities, they named these groups not as "kids" but as members of a special group. Hence their behavior got singled out. She also found that members of marginalized social groups were much more likely to have their actions interpreted as violent according to the criteria of "too much force." A certain degree of force that did not cross the line into "too much" was always considered okay. But much lower degrees of force used by girls were likely to draw the interpretation of violence.

The alternative to the interpretation of violence as too much force is based on an interpretation of what is violated, as noted above—for example, a person's rights or his or her ability to act. This leads to a wider appreciation of violence than does an interpretation based on the excessive use of force. It includes a focus on the social position of individuals and how that position may be used to exercise power over others. In this version of violence, the process of domination is more important than the amount of force used. Included are intimidation, threats, and emotional abuse as well as physical harm. Some of these practices are silent, barely visible, and easily overlooked by teachers. But they produce harm and sometimes impact more powerfully on victims than does physical force. Text message bullying and postings on social networking sites are examples of the kind of action that can violate another person without crossing the usual thresholds of "too much force." Likewise, the individual (teacher or student) who walks up to and stands over a student with his nose two inches from the victim's face and shouts at the student and intentionally elicits fear without ever touching the student might also be said to violate the personhood of the victim.

Howard Zehr (1990, 2002), in his work on restorative justice, invites us to make another shift in how we think of violence. He suggests that the focus of the law (and, by analogy, official school policy) has for too long been on the enforcement of rules and of authority and not enough on what happens to people in relationships. For Zehr, an act of aggression should be considered in terms of the harm done to a relationship. He asks us to think in more relational terms about offending behavior. The major implication of this shift in thinking lies in the response to the offense.

Rather than restoring the authority of the rules or the status of those in authority, Zehr advocates that we think more about *addressing the harm done to a relationship and setting that right.* The result might be the development of responses that produce changes in relationships in the school community, rather than instituting punishments that are actually less likely to effect behavior change.

So violence, as we are referring to it, is a practice of power that violates a relationship with another person. We should remember, though, that not all practices of power are violent. Power, in the terms articulated by Michel Foucault (2000), is the often quite ordinary property of a relation in which one person tries to influence another. To be called violent, it usually has to contain an element of an effort to dominate another against his or her will.

ANTECEDENTS TO VIOLENCE

Violent responses in conflict situations do not happen by chance, or even as a result of individual personal qualities. In this book, we stand on the following principle (explained more fully in Chapter 2): *The person is not the problem; the problem is the problem.* This means that we might profitably look for the antecedents to violence in a relational or cultural context rather than in the psychological makeup of the central perpetrator.

One line of inquiry might be into the social and cultural norms at work in the lives of students. Such norms are often laid down as pieces of discourse that are simply assumed without question. They are the taken-for-granted assumptions on which people routinely act without having to give the matter too much thought. They can be expressed as discursive statements. Here are some examples.

If you don't fight when challenged, you must be weak.

If you are going to become a man, you have to toughen up.

If you come onto our territory, then you are asking for a fight.

In my culture, you fight first and ask questions later.

Boys who refuse to fight must be gay.

I won't start a fight but, if someone else does, I will finish it.

It is important to get in the first punch.

These discursive statements have implications for how we might address conflict situations. It is important, for example, to substitute alternative pieces of discourse for those that support violent resolutions. These alternative pieces of discourse need to have meaning for young people and not just for adults. That is, they need to be found in the cultural world in which young people live. For example, here are some alternative discourses to those above:

> A real man is respectful of women and does not use violence to dominate them.

> It takes more courage sometimes not to fight.

> I don't care whether you think I am gay or not. Gay people have just as much right to live in peace as you do.

> I will defend myself if attacked, but I will never initiate violence.

> I believe in nonviolence and respect for differences between people.

These are just examples. There will always be such alternative discourses available to young people in a language community. The challenge for school leaders is to identify alternative discourses and bring them into the light, so that young people can choose to stand upon them. They must first be elicited, made known, and supported in action.

Another antecedent to violence is the defining of belonging and identity in relation to the control of territory. We can think of territory quite literally as physical space—that is, as neighborhoods, streets, or areas of a classroom and a schoolyard. Or in more abstract terms, territory can be the space taken up, or not allowed to be taken up, in a conversation.

Understanding how conflict emerges among young people in a school often means understanding the dynamics of community territories. "This is our space. Stay out of it!" Students often want to say this about neighborhoods, corners of the schoolyard, or seats in a classroom. Contests over territory lead to actions being perceived as threats to territorial belonging.

We can understand these territorial dynamics in terms of identity narratives. Identity is always formed in relation to others, in conversation with those who matter to us. And it is formed in relation to narratives that move through time but which are also anchored in space. Everyone develops personal identity through some sense of belonging to a reference group, or to a membership club (White, 2007).

It is tempting to resort to ethological explanations of human conflict and to refer to animal species for which territorial struggle occurs daily. Human territorial struggles are just like cat fights, we could say. Human beings are, of course, similar to other animals in this regard. But they are also different in key respects. Human beings have the ability to define territory in more abstract terms than cats. Our territories are therefore infinitely more flexible and negotiable than those of other animal species. We can thus do what philosopher Gilles Deleuze (Deleuze & Parnet, 2002) proposes and *deterritorialize* and then *reterritorialize*. This possibility provides a focus for *conflict resolution* work. We can invite people into conversations in which contested territories are redefined in more flexible terms and renegotiated.

Other antecedents to violence lie in the processes of social dominance and power. These processes are always going to happen in some form in human communities. Michel Foucault (2000) showed how social dominance is a by-product of ongoing struggles over power relations. In the modern world, this often stops short of outright violent coercion and utilizes the more sophisticated technologies of "normalizing judgment" and the location of persons on some kind of normal curve. Striving to be normal is now critically important for the life chances of any person. The problem is that any definition of normality automatically creates a group that is assigned to the margins and required to take up a marginal identity. Such people are excluded from some aspects of modern life. The internal experience of such processes of marginalization is one of *alienation*.

Take a look at the words of Cho Seung-Hui (such as in the Wikipedia entry for him, which includes his rationale in his own words), who shot and killed 32 students in tragic circumstances at Virginia Tech in April 2007, and you will find multiple expressions of "alienation" from his peers. The same is frequently true of other mass murderers who are often described as "loners." That is, they are alienated, or estranged, from others and have lost the sense of connection that might otherwise bring about some empathy for the suffering they are causing people.

At much lower levels of seriousness, many young people find themselves alienated from learning opportunities by experiencing repeated failure in school. Or they are so often in trouble that they have learned to "switch off" to the concerns of authorities and are thus alienated from the official purpose of schooling.

Alienation is thus a common experience of school that plays a role in the production of conflict. It results from processes of social exclusion or marginalization. If we take it seriously, there are implications for conflict resolution. Processes of conflict resolution should seek to knit people back into the social fabric. They should work to be inclusive rather than exclusive, even of those who make this hard. They should be relational rather than focused on the individual as a site of pathology.

Finally, in this list of antecedents to conflict, stereotyping deserves mention. The word *stereotype* commonly refers to a conventional but simplistic idea founded on a distorted assumption about a person or a group. It is based on prejudice or dominant discourse rather than accurate data, and it is often resistant to challenge by countervailing information. The danger of stereotypes is that they are often standardized into the popular lexicon and, as a result of constant repetition, become widely believed. Stereotypes develop around racial or ethnic groups, around gender or sexual orientation, around membership of a neighborhood or social class, or around others' religious beliefs. They are primarily a form of lazy thinking.

They can be negative or positive, but it is usually the negative stereotypes that are problematic. Problems develop when people are unfairly typecast by the application of a stereotype such that possibilities for living become limited. Because they are well-known by both the members of the stereotyped group and by those who do the stereotyping, quick reactions are readily available. Repetition of stereotypes often serves as a flash point for the expression of conflicts that have been brewing for some time. Stereotyping thus can contribute to a default to violence.

Analyzing the contribution made by stereotyping to conflict within a school can lead to specific forms of conflict resolution. Deliberate efforts can be made to address the falsehoods implicit in common stereotypes, for example, through lessons that invite students to think more carefully.

PREPARATION FOR DEMOCRACY

If the arguments for addressing conflict sound like a poor recipe for schooling students to live in a dictatorship, then this is deliberate. In a democratic society, students should be prepared to become citizens of a democratic social world. A democracy is not just a society where elections take place to choose leaders; it is one where people can have a say in the shaping of their own lives. Having a say does not mean complete sovereignty for each individual. No person is that much of an island. It can mean participation in relations of power so that no one is subject to outright domination, without rights, or devoid of a voice that can be heard by others.

We are also not advocating that schools should be restructured to make them more like democracies. School administrators and teachers are charged with a leadership role in which they need to make decisions and be accountable for those decisions. We do not want to overturn this situation. But there are many things about their lives in school in which students can have a say. Not to invite them to do so risks fostering alienated citizens who will later engage in socially destructive crime. Modern democratic societies require their citizens to be literate, to be able to manipulate numbers, to understand the scientific method, and to develop an appreciation of their social and historical context. Meeting these requirements is the task of curriculum design, and no one would dispute them. Schools are, however, also places where children should learn how to get along with others, how to regulate their personal desires and preferences in relation to the common good, and how to handle differences with others in an inclusive way.

Children do not automatically know how to participate in social interactions of these kinds. They have to learn the skills involved. Schools, therefore, have to *scaffold* (in Vygotsky's [1986] terms) the development of the attitudes and practices that will sustain democracy. These lessons have been called the implicit hidden curriculum of schooling (McLaren, 2005), but we are recommending that they be made explicit. Julia Gillard (2010), the first woman elected prime minister of Australia, in her prior role as Minister of Education, spelled out explicitly the significance for education of dealing with conflict and violence.

> [T]o reach our highest expectations, we need to understand one simple proposition: happier and safer schools are better schools; and happier and safer students are more successful students.
>
> The benefits of increased student wellbeing are well known. It has a direct impact on academic achievement through greater levels of engagement with schooling, better classroom behaviour and a greater sense of classroom ethos and togetherness. The higher the level of a student's wellbeing, the higher their retention levels and year-12 results tend to be and this has very positive effects on economic goals like productivity, social inclusion and the building of social capital.
>
> So improving wellbeing and eliminating bullying aren't side issues, they are major educational goals for the nation. (p. 2)

Democracy in this sense is always, to some degree, out of reach, always a promise of a future that we are reaching toward. But it is no less an important idea because of that. It involves always staying in conversation with people, rather than shutting down conversation in favor of *monological thinking*. By contrast, *dialogical thinking* is endlessly creative, always producing new forms of difference through remaining open to multiple perspectives.

SUMMARY

In this chapter, we have laid out some of the working assumptions of the book. These include the idea that conflict is normal. It results from the expression of differences between people. But violence does not have to be normalized. It needs to be addressed in ways that effectively stop it and deal with any harm that has already been done.

We have also explained why punitive zero tolerance policies do not work. Empirical evidence suggests that they fail to reduce levels of violence in schools. So what is to be done? Our argument throughout this book will be for the implementation of a comprehensive range of practices in a matrix that can be chosen from to address different kinds of situations.

We have also discussed some of the background discourses that affect how we think about conflict and violence. Too often, people's working definitions focus on "too much force" rather than on the violation of a person's rights. The latter emphasis makes creating learning situations in schools where conflict is addressed constructively a basic lesson in citizenship for a democratic society.

In this chapter, we have briefly mentioned the narrative perspective that will permeate this book. In Chapter 2, we shall spell this perspective out in more detail.

QUESTIONS FOR REFLECTION

1. In a school, what actions constitute violence that cannot be accepted as normal?

2. Can you identify instances of violence in which someone's rights were violated despite "too much force" not being present?

3. How are boys and girls responded to differently with regard to violence?

4. What is your personal style of responding to conflict? How did you learn that?

5. When have you surprised yourself with how well you handled conflict? How do you account for these instances?

6. What forms of difference do you personally find most challenging to work with?

QUESTIONS FOR RESEARCH

1. How might we measure the success of a comprehensive approach to conflict resolution?

2. How might it be compared with a zero tolerance approach?

3. What are the most powerful and the most common antecedents to violence?

4. How do school leaders and counselors think about their role in relation to addressing conflict in schools? Do they relate it to preparing students to live in a democratic society?

2

A Narrative
Perspective

INTRODUCTION TO NARRATIVE PRACTICE

This book is written from a consistent perspective. We make no apology for that. However, it is only fair that we spell out this perspective and situate the practices outlined throughout the rest of this book within this philosophical angle. We shall now make clear the assumptions on which this book is built.

The perspective we shall highlight has become known as *narrative practice.* This is shorthand for an ethical orientation and a range of practices that draw from contemporary movements in the fields of social science, social theory, philosophy, cultural studies, social psychology, anthropology, and sociology.

It grows out of work done initially in the family therapy arena, first by Michael White of Australia and David Epston of New Zealand (White, 2007; White & Epston, 1990). The application of these principles of practice has been extended into both school counseling (Winslade & Monk, 2007) and conflict resolution (Winslade & Monk, 2000, 2008).

A narrative perspective understands social practices as narrative performances, complete with plot trajectories, prescribed characters and roles, and setting constraints. The role of stories in the construction of human behavior is taken more seriously than it has been taken traditionally in the social sciences, where stories have been regarded as second-rate sources of knowledge and the primary emphasis has been on identifying the underlying factors or forces at work beneath stories. From a narrative perspective, this emphasis is reversed on the grounds that people routinely make sense of their lives through the recounting of stories.

"How was school today?" (if it elicits more than a monosyllabic response) will lead to the telling of a story. "Tell me how your English class went" expects a narrative in response. The interview question, "What led to the fight?" would raise eyebrows if it were answered with a list of analytical causal factors, rather than with a story.

People also act upon the basis of the narratives that they form about themselves and about others. If a student is storied as a behavior problem, then he or she is often watched more closely, spoken to more sternly, and punished more severely than someone who features in the storyline of "promising leader" and "straight-A student." Therefore, there is much to be gained by examining the effects of the stories, rather than treating them as watered-down versions of the truth.

THE PERSON IS NOT THE PROBLEM

What does this mean for conflict in school communities? One implication is the understanding that students and teachers are often caught up in a problem story (organized around a conflict) rather than that they are problem persons by nature. Another way to say this is Michael White's aphorism, "The person is not the problem; the problem is the problem" (White, 1989, p. 6; Winslade & Monk, 2007). This statement expresses a principle of profound respect. It embodies a commitment to listening to people's best intentions, rather than rushing to respond to assumptions about their worst ones. It also implies understanding what people say as if they are competent moral agents, rather than deficient in some way (and therefore not to be taken as seriously).

By contrast, referring to individuals as "the problem" is rife within many schools. Individual students are responded to as, for example, "troublemakers," and their identity is shaped by the reputation that ensues. The logic that is so common is founded on the assumption that when there is trouble, it can be accounted for with reference to an assumed character deficit. This deficit can be a moral one ("She is a bad person"), a medical one ("He is attention deficit disordered"), an educational one ("She is learning disabled"), or a social one ("He is an at-risk student"). Also common in school discourse is the habit of blame-shifting. With a little more sympathy for the child, the deficit can be shifted to the parents or the family ("What can you expect when this child comes from a dysfunctional family!"). Sole-parent or divorced families are regularly assumed, on little evidence, to be deficient in their provision of care for children's upbringing.

Sometimes whole social groups of people are assigned deficit status as minorities. One African American young woman recounted to one of us how she was told that she had been designated "at risk" simply on the basis of her skin color. The assumption that she was at risk had been made on the foundation of a scientifically dubious mapping of statistics onto the life of an individual. In this assumption, little account was taken of her highly successful performance at school.

A recent tendency in the political discourse of schooling has been the growth of *deficit thinking* in relation to teachers and schools. The concept of a failing school has been repeated often enough to establish a coefficient of truth that casts a shadow over the activities of all who participate in such a school, whether the description is justified or not.

The problem with the assignment of deficit is not just whether the description is accurate or not. The bigger problem is that deficit discourse is always *reductionistic.* It totalizes persons or groups of persons and organizes thinking about an individual or a group on a narrow range of experience. People are always more complex than any single description of them. So are schools. Exceptions can always be found to any description, even the most accurate of them. The problem of assigning deficits to people lies more in the side effects that are created. Let us examine some of these.

SIDE EFFECTS OF DEFICIT THINKING

A principal side effect lies in the impact on the individual students' story of themselves. Especially when a deficit description has the authority of a teacher or principal behind it, or even more powerfully, the authority of a doctor or psychologist, it is very hard for a young person to deny. To some degree, the student has to internalize the description and become the person thus described. Another common side effect is the increased sense of personal helplessness and consequent reliance on professionals to fix problems (Gergen, 1994). The logic that builds up is like this: *If I am, if my child is, or if my student is, disordered in some way, then the problem I am having with him or her stems from some aspect of that individual's nature and there is little that I can do about it. I therefore need to seek a referral to a professional psychologist or doctor to address the problem.* This logic typically stops people from listening to or taking seriously what the person says. Often the problem is exacerbated as a result. Kenneth Gergen describes the result as "enfeebling" rather than empowering.

Why are we stressing the importance of deficit logic and totalizing in a book on conflict resolution in schools? The reason is that the totalizing of people is very common in conflict situations. It is tempting to address an issue in the relationships of a school by resorting to deficit discourse and the totalizing habit. *If I am angry with someone, there must be something wrong with her. Something in his nature explains why he is so difficult for me.* In conflict, all sorts of things are ascribed to people's nature. For example, the accusation "You are a liar!" uses the verb *to be* to fix the behavior of telling a lie indelibly in the nature of the other person and excuses the speaker from discerning the difference between truth and lies in the future.

Narrative school counselors thus typically steer clear of descriptions of young people that assign deficits to their nature or totalize their identities in a single word or phrase. Examples of such descriptions include the totalizing of individuals as "bullies" or "victims," "good students" or "bad students," "behavior problems" or "learning disabled," "at risk" or "lacking in social skills." Instead, we would start from the assumption that every person who gets involved in bullying practices or behavioral disturbances or clumsy social interactions is also capable of many other styles of relationship. No one is a bully or a victim or a behavior problem by nature.

The challenge is to make it possible, for example, for the bully, the victim, and the bystanders all to step out of the story that is performed around the practice of bullying and into another storyline that is incompatible with the continuation of bullying. Rather than essential categories of personhood, we assume that each description establishes positions in a narrative. If a narrative is thus taken up and performed, then it can also be put down and set aside by the protagonists in the story, provided that they are effectively invited to do so.

The proviso in the last clause of the previous sentence has been the goal of the development of narrative practice in schools. The issuing of such invitations to set a problematic story aside and open up a counter narrative is achieved principally by the asking of carefully designed questions. As this book develops, we shall demonstrate many examples of such questions. But these questions are not mechanical techniques. They are generated out of some philosophical assumptions.

A narrative practice emphasizes problems of violence or bullying or behavior disturbance in terms of relational patterns, rather than primarily in terms of the internal motivations and feelings of the individual participants. It does not traffic in essentialist or naturalistic explanations of individual pathology so much as in explanations of actions that rely on relational strategy. Bullying, for example, is not understood as resulting from a buildup of "anger" inside the bully, which then requires retraining in "anger management." From a narrative perspective, the bullying *relationship* is central to the practice of bullying. Bullying actions are attempts to achieve relational effects. And the bystanders who witness this relation are also part of the relational pattern. Hence, it makes sense to target that relationship for transformation directly. In Chapter 9, we shall describe an approach to bullying based on just such assumptions.

MULTIPLE STORIES

A basic assumption of narrative practice is that we are all made up of, or make ourselves out of, multiple narratives. Some have talked about the sense in which our lives in the modern world are no longer singular (for example, Gergen, 1992). These narratives often overlap and are also sometimes quite different, because they develop in diverse contexts of our lives. What is true for individuals also applies to relationships, particularly relationships that have existed over time. A relationship can also be said to have multiple stories in which it lives. One narrative of a relationship may feature conflict and another may feature peaceful relations, for example.

A concern in many psychologies has been an interest in bringing disparate narratives together in a process of integration. There has been a valuing of self-actualization that stresses becoming a singular, more congruent, finished product of a self.

Narrative practice suggests another alternative. Instead of working against the fractionalizing of identity narratives, we might celebrate it and take advantage of it. The advantage of viewing a person or a relationship as multiply storied rather than single-storied is that conflict resolution need not mean tying up all the loose ends of the conflict narrative, so much as shifting to another storyline altogether. For narrative practice, a story of peacefulness, or cooperation, or respect, or whatever description fits, need not so much grow out of the conflict story as ride alongside it. The challenge of conflict resolution, therefore, becomes inviting people to change horses and to jump across to the alternative storyline. The new storyline has its own history, which can be retrieved and strengthened, and it has its own future, which can be planned and mapped out. Once parties to a dispute have made the jump across to the new storyline, then outstanding issues can often quickly be resolved.

DOUBLE LISTENING

The assumption of alternative storylines suggests a new listening skill. It suggests that we should listen not just singly but doubly (White, 2006; Winslade & Monk, 2008). Double listening hears both the problem story and the solution story alongside each other. It leads us to both acknowledge and recognize (Baruch Bush & Folger's [1994] term) the pain of the conflict story and also the story of hope. As we engage in double listening, we hear greater complexity in what people say, sometimes even within the same sentence. We start to catch the snippets of information that are commonly glossed over as indications of the existence of another subjugated story.

Take this statement as an example: "I was really angry at the time, but I calmed down later." Most commonly, people hear this as a statement in a story of anger and outrage. Double listening enables us to also hear the story of "calmed down later." This story may contain some important preferences for a different way of interacting, for more considered reflection, for revision of the initial reaction. The word *but* in the middle of a sentence acts as a hinge around which two stories are swinging. Once we hear these two stories, we are in a position to contrast them and to invite people to make a deliberate choice between them.

Here is another example: Someone says, "I want to get on better with my math teacher, but every time she gets on my back, it really annoys me and I stop doing work for her." Double listening registers two stories again. The story of a desire to get on well with the person's math teacher is being overshadowed by the story of annoyance at the teacher who "gets on his back." If we are double listening, we can not only register the story of annoyance but also inquire into the other story and say something like, "Tell me why you want to get on better with your math teacher, and how are you trying to show her that?"

Double listening also allows us to notice contradictions between words and nonverbal expressions. Think of the situation where someone says yes to an idea but in a hesitant voice and with an unenthusiastic facial expression. Nonverbally, she may be saying no, while saying yes out loud. Which story should we respond to? Double listening suggests we should hear both the yes and the no as entry points to contradictory stories, each of which has meaning within a different narrative. Neither is the correct story, but each deserves curious inquiry.

EXTERNALIZING CONVERSATION

A regular feature of narrative conversations is the use of externalizing language (White, 2007; Winslade & Monk, 2000, 2007). This form of language is a grammatical shift in which problems or conflicts are referred to in the third person. They are spoken about as if they were objects operating as free agents in the world of the protagonists. The grammatical shift initiates a shift in thinking, not just in the grammar of sentences but also in the grammar of relationships. The implicit message is that conflicts have a life of their own. They progress along their own trajectory through a series of complications in which they trip people up and send them hurtling toward a preordained denouement.

A narrative practitioner will thus inquire not so much into how two disputants caused a conflict as into how a conflict caught them both in its web. She might follow up with questions along the lines of, "Has the conflict *invited* you to act against your better judgment?" "Is it interfering with your life?" "Is it persuading you to think about each other or to say things that don't really fit with how you would prefer to think and speak?"

Consistent use of this kind of language, in which the conflict is objectified rather than the person(s), helps avoid inadvertent blaming and interrupts the usual patterns of speech in which a conflict has been talked about hitherto. It also helps people to slowly *dis*-identify with the conflict itself. From there, they can have room to identify with a different story of relations between themselves and others. Externalizing achieves this shift potentially by separating persons and conflicts. It lines up disputing parties as alongside each other struggling against the problem, rather than lining them up as struggling against each other. In the process, externalizing allows people to save face a little.

Sometimes the development of an externalized name for a conflict simply pops up in the conversation. Someone says something like, "I am sick and tired of this whole mess." A skilled practitioner will pick up on this expression and inquire about what "this whole mess" is doing, how it is capturing both of the parties, overriding their better intentions, and causing friction in their relations. On other occasions, a conflict resolution practitioner will explicitly inquire of the parties about what they would call the conflict if they could give it a name. The trick here is to choose a name that encompasses both parties' perspectives and describes the situation, rather than the feelings associated with one side of the story. Short of a satisfactory name being chosen, we can always continue to refer to the conflict as "it," or "the problem," or "the argument," and so on.

MAPPING THE EFFECTS OF A PROBLEM

Once an externalized name for a conflict has been developed, it should be used consistently from then on. The best way to develop the logic of externalizing is to begin to map the effects of the conflict. The word *map* can be taken to be a metaphor or to indicate the literal drawing of a diagram on a piece of paper or a whiteboard. Notice here the emphasis on identifying the *effects* of the problem, rather than on identifying the *causes* of the problem.

It involves inquiry into how a person is being affected by the *conflict itself,* rather than by what the other person is doing. It thus helps the practitioner to avoid joining with any blaming logic.

Here are some sample questions that might guide an inquiry into the effects of a conflict:

- How is this conflict getting you to feel? (Rather than, How are you feeling?)
- What is this whole thing costing you?
- Is it getting you to act against your better judgment? If so, how?
- What is the argument talking you into thinking about the other party?
- How is it all impacting on your health (or studies, or relationships with others)?
- How did the fight affect other people in the class?
- If it were to keep on getting worse, where might things end up?
- What else is it doing? (This is often the most useful question of the lot.)

The purpose of such inquiries is to invite a noticing of the range and depth of the effects of a problem that has never been brought together before. It frequently galvanizes people into a firmer desire to change the direction in which things have been going when they notice these effects. The inquiry into the effects also provides opportunity to acknowledge the emotional impact of a conflict. If done in an empathetic way, being asked about the personal effects of a problem gives someone the experience of being heard. Potentially, the other party to a conflict can also offer recognition and acknowledgment. If this happens, the divisive nature of a dispute is to some extent undermined.

DECONSTRUCTION

Another feature of narrative practice is the asking of deconstructive questions. The concept of *deconstruction* was developed first by Jacques Derrida (1976). It refers to the taking apart of a story and slowing it down so that meanings that flash by in a millisecond are teased out. In narrative practice, the use of externalizing language greatly assists this deconstruction. Sometimes, however, people get the wrong idea about deconstruction. It is not about tearing anything to pieces, and it is not about analyzing factors. Derrida was explicit about deconstruction being about opening up polarities of meaning so that surplus or new meanings could emerge. He talks also about how a deconstructive impulse often already exists implicitly within polarities.

In a mediation context, deconstruction can be practiced by using questions strategically to explore the background meanings of an incident, without attributing blame to either of the protagonists. The mediator acts as a kind of archaeologist, carefully brushing away the layers in the story to discover the underlying triggers behind the violence. This is best done in the spirit of a "naive inquirer." Going back through the history of the event, the mediator seeks to understand the meanings that are driving the conflict. As these meanings are exposed, new insights into the discursive worlds of the people in the story are found, and background cultural narratives are shown to be doing their work. Cultural differences and misunderstandings are seen, not as faults or personal deficits, but as legitimate experiences that can be acknowledged and learned from. At the same time, alternative impulses toward less conflicted relationships can be released and allowed to flourish. The story in the next section illustrates how deconstruction opens up a relationship shift in a conflict situation.

A CASE VIGNETTE

Sheik was brought to the counselor (Mike) by the school nurse after the lunch break. He had been crying and was nursing a fat lip and periodically mopping up blood from a wound inside his mouth. He said he had been in a fight on the basketball court with another boy. After explaining that he wanted to understand all about the fight, the counselor told him that he had a few questions to ask before he asked the same questions of the other boy. The conversation evolved like this.

Mike: What happened on the court?

Sheik: Well, he had the basketball and I tackled him and that's when he "lost it" and started chasing me round the court. He caught up with me and collared me and I collared him and he punched me in the mouth. I punched him a few times and he hit me back. Most of the students who were there stepped in and held us back from each other. It's just as well, because I really wanted to smash him.

Mike: Did you have a problem with this guy before the fight?

Sheik: No. We are mates and we play every lunchtime. This is the first time it's happened.

On the surface, it seemed a simple enough conflict about a basketball, but Mike had an idea that there was more to it. He wondered about the significance of the tackle that had immediately preceded the chase and the subsequent punching.

Mike: What kind of tackle was it? Isn't basketball a noncontact game?

Sheik: I was just joking around and I grabbed him around the waist like in rugby. He quickly passed the ball to another guy and then he came after me. He collared me.

Mike: What was bad about being "collared" like that?

Sheik: He grabbed my Koran.

Sheik spoke in a voice so low that Mike could hardly hear him. Mike had an idea that he was talking about a religious icon of some sort.

Mike: What was bad for you about him grabbing that?

Sheik lifted his head proudly and reached down inside his blood-covered shirt. He pulled out the thin red cord that was around his neck and on the bottom of it was a tiny replica of what appeared to be a holy book.

Sheik: See, it's my Koran. My mother gave it to me and I am not allowed to take it off. She said that if it touches the ground, I will go blind. When that kid collared me, he grabbed my Koran. No one is allowed to touch our Korans. I was scared he would tear it off and it would hit the ground. My father is in Afghanistan. We have prophets and our prophets gave us Korans.

Mike: What does your Koran say about fighting at school?

Sheik: We are not allowed to fight. We have to be peace. We aren't allowed to make trouble. I just want to peace it with Abiel.

Mike: What say I ask Abiel to come in and we can hear how the fight was for him? Let's see if we can find out what he was thinking as the fight was happening.

Abiel came through the door and Mike motioned for him to sit down. He looked away from Sheik, and his face was red and tense. Mike suspected he was feeling very angry.

Mike: Please sit down, Abiel. We need to talk about what happened on the basketball court.

Abiel: We were all playing fine and then he tackled me round the waist.

Mike: Did he break a rule?

Abiel: It's basketball! You are not supposed to touch each other! I got so mad that he was giving me a rugby tackle.

Mike: Sheik said that he collared you when you collared him. What was bad about that?

Abiel: He was ripping my buttons. My mum hates it when my clothes are torn. She said that she would give me a hiding if my shirt gets ripped.

Neither of the two boys was aware of the significance of what had just been revealed. Here were two stories about their respective mothers being exposed and how they therefore had to defend themselves. They had obligations to protect those they loved and were, therefore, prepared to ignore the school sanctions and consequences for fighting.

Mike took a deep breath and continued. He looked over at Sheik who was still trying to stop the flow of blood.

Mike: Sheik, would you please explain to Abiel why you got so mad when he collared you?

Sheik: It's because you touched my Koran. [*He reached inside his shirt and pulled out the red cord that held his Koran.*] My mother gave this to me and she told me that if it touches the ground, I go blind. I thought you were going to rip it off me. It's 'cause of the prophets.

Abiel: I didn't know about the Koran. All I was thinking about was getting you to stop ripping my shirt. I am sorry I punched you.

Sheik: I am sorry I tackled you. I was only joking around.

Mike: It seems as if neither of you wanted to fight, but both of you had things that you believed in and things to defend. What kind of relationship with each other would you rather have?

Abiel: We can be friends.

Mike: And you, Sheik?

Sheik: Yeah, I didn't want to fight. I am not really allowed to fight.

(He reached over to shake Abiel's hand.)

Abiel: All "goods."

Abiel raised his head slightly in response to Sheik's offer of peace. Mike knew that the boys had made their peace through these subtle gestures.

Mike: Tomorrow we will meet again first thing in the morning to work out how we are going to tell others who saw the fight that we have made long-term peace. I want you to think of the best ways to do this tonight, and I would like you to tell your parents about the fight and how you have sorted it out. I will call them tomorrow afternoon and explain how mature you have been in solving this problem, but I want to give you a chance to do this first yourselves.

Mike met with the two boys the next morning.

Mike: How did it go with your parents?

Sheik: That was the hardest thing to do. I didn't want to tell my mum. I knew she'd be angry and at first she was angry, but when I told her about what Abiel said about his shirt being ripped and how we sorted it out, she calmed down. My brother said I done good.

Abiel: My mum was the same because I am not allowed to fight. She said there's too much hating in the world. My dad left us because of fighting. I think she was proud of me for sorting it out.

Mike: What should we tell all those observers and how should we do it?

Sheik: We don't need to say anything. We'll just play basketball again as if nothing happened.

Abiel: Yeah, it's over now. They won't say anything and if they do want to "rark it up" [provoke us] we will let them know.

APOLOGIES

Sometimes people assume that giving an apology ends the matter. When the two boys shook hands and Abiel said, "All goods," the apology may have been genuine and all that was needed for the conflict to be resolved. Among teenagers at this school, the term is widely used to signify the end of conflict. However, their peer group may not want the conflict to be resolved and may actively provoke further trouble. There can be endless entertainment for witnesses to these kinds of disputes.

From a narrative perspective, however, an apology is an event in a story. If we stop to consider how it fits within a larger relational story, it no longer assumes the position of ending the process. We find it more useful to understand an apology as the initiation of a new storyline. Rather than the end of something, it can be the beginning of something. The challenge is to ask further questions at this stage to generate further elaboration of the story of peace.

We should caution against apologies as requirements, however. Students need to arrive at the desire to make an apology of their own free will rather than be coerced into doing so. They may be asked if they are ready to set things right and may proffer an apology in response. For others, an acknowledgment that they have done something problematic may be as far as they are prepared to go. Such acknowledgments should also be graciously accepted and treated as the start of a new story.

On this occasion, the counselor helps to cement in the effects of the apology by involving the others in recognizing and supporting the development. He sets out a plan by which the observers to the fight and those who held the two boys back and prevented it escalating can be included in the new storyline. This line of accountability is extended to the families of the boys, and he sets a test for them to include their parents in the reconstruction of their broken relationship. By advising the boys that he will call their parents to reinforce their good work in problem solving and conflict resolution, he adds a significant number of people to the audience of change, thereby increasing the likelihood that the apology will hold and that the meaning of it will continue to be performed.

This plan contains a number of key features. Firstly, it is detailed; secondly, it is limited in time; and thirdly, it is possible for the boys to carry out. It may be hard, but it is possible. He ensures that the boys do the talking to their parents in their own way, and he invites them to think further about the best ways to tell the others who witnessed the violence.

DEVELOPING A COUNTER STORY

As well as illustrating the deconstruction of the meaning of an action (the "tackle" or the "collaring"), this story illustrates the move from a conflict story to a story of resolution. In narrative terms, this story is referred to as the "counter story" (Lindemann Nelson, 2001). It runs counter to the direction of the conflict story. In this instance, the deconstruction of the reactions of each boy is made clear and heard by the other. Mike is then able to move into the creation of a counter story. Once he has invited the boys to step across into this storyline, it gathers its own momentum and heads off into a different future.

The opening of this counter story begins with Mike asking the two boys, "What kind of relationship with each other would you rather have?" In their responses, they reference a story of being friends and of not wanting to fight. Like the conflict story, the counter story has a history and a future, as well as a present. The history involves being friends before this incident and making a commitment to their respective mothers about protecting the Koran and the shirt. The future lies in the promise of the apology and the efforts made to sew it into the fabric of their relationship. Fronting up to their family members and friends are significant plot elements in the evolution of this story.

There are, however, a variety of ways in which such a counter story can be opened up. Double listening can uncover elements of a preferred story, even early in a conversation. Exceptions to the problem story (for example, "Until yesterday we used to be friends") can be thrown into the middle of a conversation and developed by being inquired into. Disputants can be asked directly whether they like what the conflict is doing and if they would mind if it continued to get worse. If someone says, "No I don't like it," she then can be asked what she would prefer. Any preference for peaceful relations or respect and understanding (for example) can serve as the opening to a counter story. This story is always likely to have a history and a future, as well as a present, each of which can be inquired into.

The counter story can be developed further by exploring people's reasons for not wanting a conflict to worsen and for preferring something else. In the process, conversations can open up about people's cherished values, personal commitments, and cultural resources. For example, many people personally nurture relational ideals of cooperation with others, fair and just negotiation, resistance to cultural colonization, democratic decision making, hope for a peaceful future, caring for others, and so on. Under the influence of a conflict-saturated story, such value commitments can be consigned to the shadows. To harbor such values while acting in ways that contradict them does not make a person a hypocrite. It merely indicates the existence of multiple stories. It is a hallmark of narrative practice to facilitate the expression of people's best selves and noblest intentions, rather than to allow conflict stories to dominate the field of interaction. What is created in the contrasting of conflict stories with counter stories is the expansion of the freedom to choose something different. When conflict resolution is practiced effectively according to these principles, people experience not being locked in to a conflict so tightly. The grip of a conflict story is loosened. Other futures open up. Exercise of this freedom potentially creates a community in which learning takes place—not just learning how to complete math problems and practice language arts but learning how to be a good citizen in a school community and beyond.

SUMMARY

We have outlined in this chapter the basic principles of respect on which a narrative practice is built. We have also outlined the steps in a narrative practice of conflict resolution:

1. Practicing double listening to a conflict story

2. Developing an externalizing conversation

3. Mapping the effects of a conflict

4. Deconstructing the meaning of the conflict story

5. Opening a counter story that heads off on a trajectory that is incompatible with that of the conflict story

6. Giving the counter story a history and a future as well as a present

7. Understanding the counter story as an expression of what people give value to and hope for

8. Developing options for resolution out of the counter story

These principles and features of a method will be embodied in slightly different ways in each of the chapters that follow. Each of these chapters will outline a different approach to conflict resolution, each designed for a different variety of context or a different manifestation of a problem. The principles will, however, remain constant because they are expressions of a consistent philosophy.

A key idea is the ethical principle of looking at persons respectfully, as worthy of respect in their own right, rather than thinking of them in terms of a deficit assumption. *The person is not the problem; the problem is the problem.* This aphorism is so important that we shall refer to it a number of times.

QUESTIONS FOR REFLECTION

1. What stood out for you about the narrative perspective?

2. How have you personally experienced being assigned a deficit description? What effect did this have? How did you accept it, or fight against it, or both?

3. What difference does it make to think of each person's life as featuring multiple stories rather than as single-storied?

4. Reflect on the expression, *The person is not the problem; the problem is the problem.* What are its implications?

5. What difference does it make to think of an apology as the start of a story rather than as the end of one?

QUESTIONS FOR RESEARCH

1. How might research studies into problems in schools be different if they always took into account the existence of counter stories?

2. How can deconstruction be used as a research tool?

3. What might be learned from the collection of an archive of school conflict narratives?

4. What are the effects of a fight in a school on those immediately involved and on others?

3

Counseling

COUNSELING IN SCHOOLS IS ABOUT LEARNING, NOT CURE

Much of the work of conflict resolution needs to take place in conversations between people. If conflict is a relational phenomenon, then it makes sense that conflict resolution needs to focus on the relational dimensions of people's lives. But that is not to say that much conflict resolution work cannot be done through counseling individuals. Students in schools can fruitfully talk over with a counselor how they are going to approach a relational context, either to avoid a full-blown conflict emerging or to address one that has already arisen.

It is necessary, however, to pause and consider just what counseling is and how conflict resolution work can fit within a counselor's practice. In educational contexts, we would submit that counseling is primarily not about "cure" but about "learning and development," especially about learning how to live and relate to others. (We shall leave aside for now the question of whether counseling should best be thought of this way in clinical contexts as well.) If, in schools at least, it is not about cure, then it should not focus on a medical model of diagnosing deficits and "treating" these. Such metaphors do not fit with education and seldom aid the task of learning how to live. There is an increasing trend to introduce medical discourse into schools, and we believe that both counselors and administrators should resist it. This might mean refusing to see behaviors of students as sufficiently explained by medical diagnoses such as attention deficit disordered or conduct disordered. It is not even necessary to see these diagnoses as wrong. They just have limited usefulness in the school setting. They are often understood as totalizing descriptions with many unintended side effects, and they can blind everybody to what lies outside their explanatory value. They can also bind administrators into simplistic remedies such as learning a few tricks of "anger management" in order to appease teachers and parents.

If we start from the assumption that counseling in schools is about helping students learn how to live in a school community and to negotiate their pathway through a school career, then there is a place for counseling in conflict resolution. It is about helping students construct lives amid the differences they encounter with others. In the end, conflict is about difference, and one of the most important challenges faced by people in the modern world lies in learning how to negotiate their relationships with difference.

Much counseling work is about helping people work through personal struggles in relation to identity stories. Such counseling is less related to mediation than to conflict coaching. In this chapter, we focus on several aspects of counseling that should be considered a core part of the overall program of managing conflict in a school context. If school administrators are aware of these counseling purposes, then they are better positioned to use school counselors' or psychologists' skills by referring individuals for such assistance. And if school counselors and psychologists are aware of these specific purposes, then they can offer them as options for students (and sometimes teachers and administrators too) when the need arises.

CONFLICT COACHING

Conflict coaching is a relatively new development in the conflict resolution literature (see Brinkert, 2006; Jones & Brinkert, 2008). It grows out of management coaching and mentoring, which makes sense, considering that a large part of the role of a manager involves the management of conflict in organizations. This is no less true in schools than in other kinds of organizations. If sufficient trust develops between a school principal and a counselor, the latter can be called upon by the administrator to act in a coaching role to assist in the management of the conflicts that inevitably develop in schools. School counselors can also act as consultants for teachers, coaching them in the management of relationships in the classroom.

Then there are the students. School counselors often hear students complain about teachers or about other students. Each of these complaints represents a learning opportunity for those involved. Often the most useful option is to bring the two parties together for a mediation session or possibly a restorative conversation. Perhaps the relationships among a whole class are affected and a circle conversation seems like the method of choice. These approaches will be outlined in subsequent chapters in this book. Sometimes, however, the complainant does not want to sit down with the other party to the conflict. Sometimes, too, the other party is not willing to participate in a joint meeting. The complainant may also wish to take personal responsibility for addressing a relationship problem and simply needs some support to do so. In each of these situations, conflict coaching may be the method of choice.

When fielding a complaint from a student about a teacher, for example, here is a possible conversation sequence.

"So you are unhappy with what this teacher said or did. Right?"

"Yes."

"Would you like to tell me the story of what happened?"

The student tells the story, and the counselor listens carefully and then summarizes what she has heard.

"If I understand you correctly, your relationship with your teacher is not how you would like it to be, and you would like things to be different."

"Yes." [Sometimes some work is needed to get to this yes, especially if the student is convinced that the problem lies in the person of the teacher rather than in the relationship. We would stress again here the importance of working from the principle that *the person is not the problem; the problem is the problem.*]

"So it seems to me that there are at least three possible options for how we could go on from here. One: You can tell me the story of what happened, much as you have done, get it off your chest, and that might be enough. You can go away and figure out what to do yourself. Two: We could talk here without the teacher joining us, and we could work on how you might improve things from your side of the relationship. If you want to repair any harm that has been done, we can look at ways to do this. We could also develop strategies for you to work on, even strategies for making your teacher into a better teacher for you [the conflict coaching option]. Three: I could invite your teacher to meet here with you, and we could talk together about how to address this problem in your relationship [the mediation option]. Which of these three approaches are you interested in? Or do you have another idea?"

If the student opts for the second option, then the counselor needs to implement a conflict coaching strategy.

NARRATIVE CONFLICT COACHING

There are several published models of conflict coaching, each reflecting a different theoretical orientation (Jones & Brinkert, 2008). Here we want to elaborate a narrative model. This is partially outlined by Jones and Brinkert, but here we want to take it a few steps further.

First, some principles need to be reiterated. A narrative approach to conflict coaching starts from the assumption that conflict is embedded in competing narratives about what has happened. It also assumes that these narratives will be shaped by a process of selection from out of the range of possible plot elements and that there are always possible narratives that can be developed other than the conflict-saturated one. The conflict narrative that dominates will likely be held in place by power relations of some kind, particularly as expressed through some dominant discourse. In the shadows of the dominant story will always exist some other possible stories, some of which the person consulting the counselor will prefer to what has been happening. The aim of conflict coaching will be to help the person separate himself from the dominant conflict-saturated story and grow some preferred story of relationship with the other party. The assumption is that a relationship change will occur if this narrative shift takes place.

Listening to the Story

The first step in a conflict coaching conversation is to listen carefully to the story of what has happened. This involves listening for the plot events, the characterizations of people, and the thematic elements being emphasized. It involves hearing the events being told as a selection out of all the possible stories that could be told and as a particular arrangement of these story elements. That is what a narrative is. Narrative practice also alerts us to the need to practice double listening, that is, to listen for the gaps, contradictions, exceptions, and expressions of resistance to the dominance of the conflict, as well as to the conflict-saturated narrative itself. These unique outcomes will later become entry points to a possible alternative story, but at first they should simply be noted and saved for later.

As this conversation develops, the counselor should ask questions for clarification, provide acknowledgment of personal feelings expressed, and summarize what has been said. She should also begin to use externalizing language to ascribe what has happened to the problem, rather than to the persons involved. An account of the problem story and the various contributing forces at work in its production needs to be developed.

Some people come into this process with a coherent account already rehearsed. Others need to be asked lots of questions in order to generate a degree of coherence (see Cobb, 1994) in their story. This is especially likely to be true of younger people, as well as of those who have seldom been asked to speak for themselves (except for situations when they are in trouble). Teachers, on the other hand, are much more likely to be articulate in detailing their story and to present it in organized paragraphs. The difference is not one of intelligence so much as practice. Those who come from backgrounds where they have never learned storytelling skills may start by mentioning a few brief facts about events from the middle of the story. The counselor then needs to help them assemble a narrative out of a jumble of plot events. The manner in which the counselor asks the questions must be curious and "naïve," rather than inquisitional. This purpose of helping to build coherence into a story should not be underestimated in its importance. It represents a very useful coaching function, and it is about increasing a person's agency in the situation.

Here are some examples of questions that can be asked to generate an account of the conflict. A conflict coach needs to develop a range of questions in his repertoire to be called on in this stage of the process.

1. Tell me how this conflict developed. What were the main actions that you and the other person took in the development of this conflict?

2. When did this conflict first start? What were things like between you before that?

3. Was there a certain point at which things started to change, or was there a gradual shift?

4. How did the conflict take over your relationship?

5. What has contributed to making this problem as big as it has gotten?

6. Help me understand how you came to choose to do that and what it led the other person to do next.

7. How did you respond? How did he respond? And how did you respond to that?

Inquiring Into Complexity

After the basic plot elements of the story have emerged, it is useful to stretch the scope of the narrative by asking some questions that require the person to step out of her initial perspective and build a more complex account. In mediation, this complexity comes from the inclusion of the other party's account, but in conflict coaching it has to be achieved through imagining what the other person would say, or at least through inviting a bird's-eye view of the conflict story. The aim of these questions is not to invite the person to abandon her own perspective, or to take responsibility for making the other person happy, so much as to introduce greater complexity into the picture, because greater complexity increases the possibility of new story elements appearing. Here are some examples of questions that can help achieve this purpose.

1. How would you describe the pattern of interactions between you?

2. What were you assuming, and what do you imagine the other person was assuming?

3. If X were here with us, what do you think she would say about what you told me? Would she stress anything differently than you?

4. What would you hope would come out of all this, and what do you imagine the other person would be hoping for?

5. If you were X, what would you say about what you just said?

6. If someone else were watching all this happen, what would it have looked like to him?

7. How does what you did fit with the kind of person you want to be, and how does what she said fit with her kind of person?

8. From what you said, I am struggling to understand why she might have said that. Can you help me understand at all?

9. What do you think Ms. Jacobs would have to be sure of in order to be a more understanding teacher for you?

These questions, which open up greater complexity, are deconstructive of simplistic, thin accounts of a problem story. Deconstructing the story of the conflict makes it possible for students to expose and challenge the usefulness of the taken-for-granted assumptions about their relationships with others. They are offered the position of researcher into their own lives and can explore the effects of particular ways of thinking. We do not suggest that they can somehow extract themselves from their culture or from the plot of any story, nor do we think that they can somehow cut themselves adrift from the structures and rules of the school.

However, as they become more understanding of the subtle pressures and expectations that accompany a reputation or an identity, they become freer to consider other options, ones that make it easier to get along with others. This process of unpacking the story further helps young people to monitor the effects of their ways of thinking and acting and opens up more possibilities for growth and development.

A CASE VIGNETTE

A student was referred to the counselor because he had been expelled from a science class by a teacher who had a reputation for excellent teaching practice. She was a newly trained teacher who had recently emigrated from India. New Zealanders affectionately refer to themselves as Kiwis. The student had told his teacher that she was not a kiwi and was accused by the teacher of being racist. When he was thrown out of the class, he couldn't understand it. He never wanted to go back to her class again, even though he enjoyed science and had previously related well to this teacher. He had a reputation for being a comedian, but the counselor was surprised to hear that she had made such a serious accusation.

"What happened that got you kicked out of class?" the counselor asked.

"We were having a good lesson and everyone was happy and working together. We were studying kiwis [a native New Zealand bird] and what happens to them at night," the student explained. "She said that kiwis are birds that sleep at night, and I was just joking around and I got a bit cheeky and said, 'How would you know? You're not a kiwi.' She really told me off and said that I had no right to tell her that she doesn't belong here and she sent me out of class. I don't know what I've done wrong."

The counselor guessed that she had thought that his comment was about her nationality and that the boy had not made this connection.

"Did you know that she is a new teacher from India?" the counselor asked him.

"Yes," he said.

"What do you think she might have thought you meant when you said, 'You're not a kiwi'?"

He thought for a moment and then said with a smile, "Now I get it. She thought I meant that she wasn't a Kiwi, so she doesn't belong here. But I meant that she wasn't a bird!"

"What do you think you need to do now that you know what your teacher was thinking?" I asked.

"I will apologize to her when I go to her class. She's a good teacher. I just didn't realize that she would take it that way."

Naming the Problem

The task of developing an externalizing conversation is aided by developing an agreed-upon name for the problem story. From then on, this name can be used as a name for the problem. Using this name repeatedly allows the counselor to avoid joining unhelpfully with either party's version of events. This is especially important when the story you have been listening to is bristling with blame. The key thing is that the name should be generated between the counselor and the client. It should not be a case of the counselor saying, "I've got an idea of what we should call this."

Sometimes a name for the problem just pops up in the conversation. On other occasions, some work needs to be done to settle on a name. It is always possible to fall back on a generic name, such as the "conflict," or the "problem," or indeed "it." There is nothing wrong with this, and such names should be used when nothing else seems appropriate. But a more apt name can perhaps be found with a little persistence, so that the "problem" becomes known as the "last period struggle," or the "argument cycle," or the "physics situation," or something else.

The key thing about an appropriate name is that it should not refer to a person but to a situation. Nor should it refer to what is happening in one person's emotional experience. For example, "anger" is not a very useful name because it is located inside one person and is not inclusive of both parties' experience of what is happening. Nor is a name liked "picking on me" very useful because it places all the responsibility for the actions implicated in the problem story on one person's shoulders. In fact, it actually leaves the speaker in a powerless position. The name, therefore, needs to be something that is inclusive of more than a single person's perspectives.

Here are some questions that can be asked to help generate a name for the problem story:

1. So if we were to think of a name for this thing that we are up against, what might we call it?

2. What could we call this situation that is causing all these problems between you both?

3. So what is it that is happening? Is it an argument? Or a tension? Or an ongoing irritation? Or what? What would you call it?

4. If we were to describe how your relationship with this teacher is, how could we describe it in a word or two and refer to it in the future without having to tell the whole story over again?

Mapping the Effects of the Problem

Once a name has been settled on, the externalizing conversation needs to advance through using it consistently. It does not particularly matter whether the client uses the assigned name herself, although many will catch on to its use. It is important that the counselor (or conflict coach) does so. The best way to build on the naming of the problem is to immediately use the name in the next few sentences and ask about "its" effects. In the process, the grammatical shift of externalizing can start to become a shift in thinking.

The aim of asking about the effects of the problem is to build up a picture of damage that the conflict is doing. Often, people are not fully aware of the extent of this damage until they answer these questions. Questions should aim for breadth of coverage of all the domains in which the problem is having an influence. This may include the domain of emotional experience ("What does it get you to feel?"), the cognitive domain ("What thoughts does it persuade you to think?"), the relational domain ("What is it getting you to say to the other person?"), the practical domains of action ("Does it get you to do anything that is out of character for you?"), and the physical domain ("Is the problem causing any physical effects in you, such as headaches, nausea, aching shoulders, lack of sleep?"). An excellent question to ask several times, after exploring some of these effects, is, "What else is it doing?"

Effects of a problematic conflict also occur in a time dimension. Therefore, we can ask about the effects that have transpired in the past, about those that are currently taking place, and about future possible effects. With regard to the latter, it is often very motivating toward some form of change to ask the following question: "If things were to keep going, and possibly get even worse than they are now, what would happen, do you think? Would you be able to stand it? What would it be like?"

Mapping the effects of the problem can also usefully extend to mapping the effects on other people, including the other party to the conflict, as well as to any bystanders or witnesses. Thinking about the effects of the problem on the other person, with whom one is in dispute, can expand the balloon of empathy and increase the motivation to resolve the dispute.

Evaluating the Effects of the Conflict

After the effects of the conflict have been sufficiently mapped, it is time to ask the student to make a judgment about these effects. Are these effects something that can be lived with, or does he want something to change? If so, how strong is the desire for change? The judgment called for is not a judgment of the other party, nor is it a judgment of himself. It is a judgment only of the problem and the work that it has done in people's lives. This question does not have to be labored over. It is enough to ask the question once and then move on. Whereas mapping the effects of the problem can usefully be lingered over for some minutes, this step is like opening a door and walking through it. When someone makes the judgment that the effects of the problem are unacceptable to her, she can be asked to elaborate by speaking to why she is making that judgment call. As she answers the "why" question, she has to take a step into her own rationale for change. Here are some examples of questions that can be used at this point in the conversation.

1. What do you think of the problem having all these effects? Is this okay with you, or does it bother you?

2. Forgive me for asking what may seem obvious, but do you mind what this problem is doing?

3. Are you able to tolerate the effects of this problem, or are you reaching the end of your tether with it?

4. What do you object to about this conflict?

5. Why don't you like what the problem has been doing?

6. Would you prefer things to be different? If so, how?

Assembling the Alternative Story

From here, the task of conflict coaching becomes one of assembling an alternative story of relationship that the person would prefer and locating it in a context where it can grow. Like any seedling, though, a fragile story needs protection from the storms of discourse by which it risks being battered. It also needs the nourishment of being fed and watered.

In conflict coaching, as distinguished from counseling for personal identity development, it is important that the focus of the conversation remains relational at this point. The important question is not, "What would you prefer for yourself?" but, "What would you prefer your relationship with the other person to be like?" Narrative practice is founded on the principle that changing the story of relationship will change the experience of it. It is not so much about achieving relationship change through the cathartic release of emotion.

The first step is to identify openings to this preferred story of relationship. Double listening will very likely have surfaced examples of such openings already. If not, they can be asked for directly. The question above, "What would you prefer?" can be followed up by further questions that locate these preferences in lived experience. "Did it used to be that way?" can locate the alternative story in the past. The more recent the past experience of the alternative story, the more helpful it can be. Long-ago experiences of a different relationship story can be too remote to be relevant.

The alternative story can also be associated with current experiences. Amid the turmoil of a conflict, people can make decisions to do something based on a different ethic or value that is not contaminated by the conflict story. They can contradict the logic of a conflict story (dedicated as it is to increasing hostility) by holding back on their worst imaginings or actions and can act in a way that would not be predicted from within the conflict story. They can harbor better intentions than they have so far made manifest.

As well as in the past or present, the impetus for an alternative story can be located in a desired future. Given the right kind of inquiry, it can be expressed as hope for something better. Such hope needs to be expressed and then fleshed out in full. As it is elaborated, expressions of hope can be realized as actions taken. Conversation can turn to ways in which possibility can be turned into reality.

DECONSTRUCTING RULES

It is often the case that conflict between young people and adults centers on arguments about "the rules." These may be family rules that a young person is bucking against in an attempt to assert her own emergent identity. They may be school rules that a young person finds irritating or cannot see the reason for. Or they may be community rules and laws that a young person falls foul of in an effort to find excitement in his life.

The conflict with an adult may often be about the policing of a rule, rather than about the rule itself. But sometimes the existence of the rule itself can seem like it is designed to oppress the person who falls foul of it. There are times when students are justified in complaining about overzealous, or selective, or vindictive policing of rules. But there are also times when the student's thinking about the rules can become rebellious in a muddled way and can lead to stands of resistance that are not well thought through.

At such times, a useful counseling conversation can focus on deconstruction of the meaning of the rules themselves and of the student's relationship with the rules. The aim of this conversation is not necessarily to coerce a person into an attitude of compliance, but to engage with the student's thinking, and to invite forward the making of choices based on considered reflection, rather than reaction. In nearly all children and young people, there is a rational and responsible story that can be grown by seeking it out through curious and compassionate questioning. Sometimes this story has not developed, simply because few adults have cared to engage with it. As a result, the student may be quite surprised to be asked and may find it awkward and difficult to hold such a conversation—all the more reason, however, to invite her into it.

The narrative principle is again that there are always multiple stories in any person and that the kind of conversation we hold makes a difference as to which story becomes prominent. Treating a person as able to think and asking questions about his thinking induces exactly the kind of thinking asked for. Treat a person as irresponsible and unable to be trusted to express a worthwhile idea, and he will surely enough fail to do the thinking that he is lamented for not doing.

Counseling conversations can play a useful role in eliciting and producing relationally responsible behavior, if pursued in the right way. To achieve this kind of purpose, a counselor must be willing to show genuine curiosity for the young person's perspective, rather than asking questions with a view to entrapping the student into a "correct" answer. In addition, school administrators need to be willing to trust a school counselor to hold such conversations in the hope of eliciting the best possible identity narrative in the student. Potentially, such conversations can be more powerful than a punishment that frequently produces the side effect of resentment.

Here are some examples of questions to open up a deconstructive inquiry about rules. Each actually represents a line of inquiry, rather than a single question.

What are the most obvious rules or strongest rules in your family?

Who applies them and how are they applied?

What are some of the rules you and your friends have?

What rules are unspoken? (Help students here to think how a rule can be unspoken. For example, say, "When someone asks you for a fight, do you always say yes, no matter what the consequences are?")

How do unspoken rules show themselves? How do they work?

Who gains the most from the rules? Who loses?

Where did these rules come from? Is there a story behind the rule? Who would know if there was?

What would happen if these rules were challenged?

What happens when people don't accept these rules?

If there were a rule that you didn't like, how would you change it?

Is there any chance you could get the school to change the rule before your suspension hearing next week?

Deconstructive conversations along these lines about the rules teenagers adhere to can highlight for students what they know but don't know that they know. Assisting them to tap into knowledge of their world in an open and curious way is immensely acknowledging and validating for students, and many say that no adult has ever talked to them like this before. Frequently, a young person will say, "I have never thought of it like that," and, "I didn't realize that she thought like that."

The impulsivity of youth and, for some, a default position of violence become reference points for rich discussions about "saving and losing face," consequences of actions, and imagining and wondering about the trajectory of a particular storyline. Looking back at the history of conflict and fighting, the identification of attitudes that support these conclusions, and conversations that dislodge the assumptions of prestige, privilege, and status, create powerful opportunities to challenge "how things are." These new sites of challenge do not come from a position of students' isolation from their school setting or their cultural background but are firmly grounded in relationships with peers, recalling remembrances of past cooperation, and alignment with what they can identify as the positive values of the school.

RESPONDING TO TRAUMA

Sometimes a school needs to support its students in their responses to a violent event. Major traumatic events can include suicides and fatal car accidents, but they also enter the realm of this book if the event that produces tragedy originates in an interpersonal crisis. We are talking here about serious attacks on individual students, school shootings, persons being threatened with weapons, rapes, sexual harassment, abuse of students by teachers, and so on. These are situations in which serious harm is done by an act of violence. In such situations, conflict resolution is not an option. For all the appealing talk about prevention being preferable, there are times when this option simply drops away and, rather than prevention, we are talking about *postvention.*

At such times, the core purpose for the existence of schools—to promote learning—is itself severely shaken, for at least some members of the school community. Suddenly, the passing of tests, the completion of homework assignments, the maintenance of a strong academic record, the desire to achieve scholastic goals, all slide down the priority list for those directly affected. What rises in importance is another kind of learning—learning how to handle a crisis as an individual and as a community. Sometimes irresponsible school leaders try to pretend that the crisis has not really happened, that this different kind of learning is not important and that the school should maintain its focus on classes, homework, and tests as if nothing has happened. More usefully, school leaders should recognize that basic needs for emotional support will, at least temporarily, take precedence over the needs for academic success for some students.

A responsible school cares about its students' and teachers' responses at such times. It offers guidance and structures pathways for responses to be channeled in the most reassuring and comforting ways possible. It pays attention to the meanings that are circulating about what has happened and takes action to manage rumor, facilitates necessary communication, enables people to face up to unpalatable truths, and fosters the kinds of meaning making that are most constructive of personal and community resilience. The roles of school administrators and counselors are very critical at such times. Many students and teachers will be looking for clear and compassionate leadership.

One of the most useful ideas is for a school to establish a crisis team to manage the crisis. This team should be made up of administrators, guidance personnel, and community leaders. Its first task should be to coordinate efforts to identify and anticipate needs of students, teachers, and parents. Once these are identified, the team should plan appropriate responses, organize the provision of counseling and other services (accessed from within or from outside the school), and provide channels through which members of the school community can talk to each other to make meaning of an event. There should be an immediate emphasis on accessing sources of comfort and stories of resilience. The general message to be conveyed to the school community is that the school is willing to confront the crisis, is not afraid of students' and teachers' responses, and is prepared to manage the situation so that suffering is responded to with caring and not unnecessarily prolonged. The school should provide guidance that enables students to learn from a difficult situation, the likes of which they have never encountered before. For example, in one school, after the death of a student, his family organized a Catholic requiem mass for his funeral. The school arranged for a Catholic member of staff to explain what would happen at the service to the students who would be attending. The crisis team should meet on a daily basis to share necessary information, respond to changing circumstances, and plan for predictable consequences of a serious event.

The role of a school counselor needs to include being a "first responder" to the traumatic effects of an event on an individual or a group of students, or even on a whole school. In order to be an effective first responder, it is necessary to bear in mind some principles of practice that will be experienced as helpful. There is a substantial literature on crisis response— sometimes called "critical incident debriefing"—and there are strong critiques of some of this literature, particularly for the frequent invitations to think about people in deficit terms and specifically with regard to the dangers associated with re-traumatizing practices. These are practices that assume that there is therapeutic value in inviting people, in the aftermath of a trauma, to enter back as fully as possible into the emotional experience of the trauma, perhaps repeatedly, in order to produce a cathartic effect or to achieve desensitization from the effects of the trauma. A narrative practice in response to the experience of trauma especially seeks to avoid the dangers of such an approach (Denborough, 2006; White, 2006). It is not possible within the space of this book to address this field in great detail, but it is possible to lay out some brief principles with a view to giving practitioners a simple framework for immediate response.

The first principle is to practice double listening (White, 2006). In this context, double listening means hearing both the distressing and negative effects of the trauma and, at the same time, listening to people's efforts to respond to the trauma in ways that give expression to what they give value to or hold precious. The assumption here is that people are not passive recipients of traumatic effects in their lives but are active in making choices about how to respond. It is still necessary to give people the opportunity to speak about what has happened and about the effects on them of a traumatic event. The value of inquiring into and mapping the effects of the trauma on a person's "sense of myself" (White, 2006, p. 27) cannot be underestimated.

A sole focus, however, on the negative effects of trauma can leave a person in a place of overwhelm and desolation that ends up magnifying these effects and making the person feel worse. On the other hand, people do many things in the face of traumatic events to make sense of them, to seek comfort from others, to reach out to others, to limit the worst effects of trauma, and to make themselves resilient. As they give testimony in counseling to the negative effects of a trauma, they might also speak of their efforts to mitigate the overwhelm and of their desire to not let it dominate them completely. Double listening hears these expressions as openings to a different story that can be developed through careful inquiry into an account of what people give value to, what they hold dear, and what sustains them through dark days.

Another key principle is to join people together in mutual support, rather than assume that people need to deal with a crisis in isolation. Facilitating group counseling, holding class meetings, and having special assemblies all have a part to play in this regard. As an alternative story of resilience is built, it needs a community of response to be scaffolded around it. Such a community can bear witness to developments in the counter story and knit them into relationships within a school community. Jones and Brinkert (2008) talk about this as assembling a "story squad." Michael White (2006) refers to "outsider witnesses" who participate in "definitional ceremonies," where they are given the chance to resonate with others' experiences.

In order to give counselors a map for immediate assistance in the face of crisis, we provide below a list of questions that can be taken as lines of inquiry. This is necessarily a short list, and we would refer counselors to other readings. These questions are drawn from several sources. We recommend Michael White's (2006) work on therapy with people affected by trauma, David Denborough's (2006) writing about community work in the face of trauma, and Wally McKenzie's (2010) article on Employment Assistance Program (EAP) counseling for people who have witnessed traumatic events.

Documenting the Trauma and Its Effects

1. Can you tell me about the trauma (or the event) that affected you?

Mapping the Effects of Trauma

2. What have been the effects of this event on your sense of yourself? On your studies? On your relationships and friendships? How has the stress been showing itself?

3. What have been some of the most difficult effects? Why have these been so difficult?

4. What changes in you have others noticed as a result of this experience?

Seeking Out the Counter Story

5. How are you enduring these effects? What are you thinking about to help you through? What memories are you holding on to?

6. Who is supporting you? Who are you reaching out to? What does this support mean?

7. Because this is so far out of the ordinary, who do you know well enough that would be willing to talk it through on a daily basis?

8. What has been the most useful thing anyone has said or done for you around this event?

9. What will be important over the next few weeks to help your mind settle again?

10. What experiences in the past have helped prepare you to handle this event?

Growing Stories of Resilience

11. Why is it important not to be completely overwhelmed by what happened?

12. How have you been successful at reducing the effects of the trauma, even temporarily? How did you learn to do this?

13. What values or commitments seem even more important to hold on to?

14. If someone else was to go through a similar experience, what advice would you give that person?

SUMMARY

This chapter has been about the role of counseling in conflict resolution. It started with the idea that counseling in schools is primarily about learning rather than cure, especially learning how to relate to others. We have outlined an approach to conflict coaching for use when counselors are working with one party to a conflict. This approach starts with double listening and proceeds with externalizing, mapping the effects of a conflict, evaluating those effects, and assembling an alternative story. We discuss also how counseling can address young people's frustration with and rebellion against rules. We advocate here for the value of a deconstructive conversation rather than an authoritarian one. Then we discuss counseling in response to traumatic events in a school community in a way that avoids re-traumatizing invitations to revisit the story of the trauma and instead focuses on building stories of resilience. We also advocate the formation of crisis teams in the aftermath of a crisis in order to manage a school community's response and to identify personal and communal needs.

QUESTIONS FOR REFLECTION

1. How have you noticed medical discourse becoming increasingly common in school discourse? What effect has this had?

2. Think of a small conflict you have experienced in a school context. Ask yourself the questions in the section on conflict coaching. What impact do you experience these questions having on you? What difference do they make?

3. Imagine a traumatic event in your school (or recall one that actually happened). Who are the key people that would be the most useful members of a crisis team to deal with this event?

4. Think of a traumatic event by which you have been affected. Work through the questions above on "seeking out the counter story" and "growing stories of resilience." Notice how these questions work.

QUESTIONS FOR RESEARCH

1. What are the totalizing discourses currently at work in schools? How might discourse analysis shed light on the work these discourses do?

2. What constitutes successful practice in the management of traumatic crises in a school?

3. How do students talk about rules at school? In their families? In their peer groups?

4

$$\overline{}$$

Mediation[*]

SEEKING OUT THE ALTERNATIVE STORY OF RELATIONSHIP

Mediation is a well-established practice in the field of conflict resolution. This chapter introduces an approach to mediation that can be learned by school counselors or by school administrators and practiced in schools. It is most useful where there is a dispute between two individuals or groups of individuals. Disputes may be between students, between teachers and students, between teachers, between teachers and parents, or between teachers and administrators. A mediator provides "negotiation assistance" (Kruk, 1997) to the disputants but leaves the decision-making power for any outcome jointly in their hands. Such outcomes may include negotiated

$$\overline{}$$

[*]A version of this chapter was published as an article in the *New Zealand Journal of Counselling* (Williams & Winslade, 2010). It is reprinted with permission.

settlements of differences or exchanges of communication that result in increased understanding without any formal agreements being needed.

It is common for both school counselors and school administrators to be approached by members of a school community who want to complain about somebody else. Often such situations call for bringing the two people together to talk through an issue. It is important for school counselors to develop the skills and frameworks of thinking necessary to perform this role. There are also many school administrators who develop considerable skill at mediating disputes. It is the aim of this chapter to provide both groups of professionals with a framework for such mediations, drawn from the application of the narrative metaphor that permeates this book.

The narrative approach to mediation (Winslade & Monk, 2000, 2008; Winslade, Monk, & Cotter, 1998) is built on a process of re-authoring a relationship story that has been caught up in a conflict-saturated story. The assumption is that people usually experience conflict stories as painful and would prefer something different. We can conceptualize this something different as an alternative relationship story that is more peaceful or understanding, or more cooperative. Mediation, therefore, involves helping people separate from the painful conflict story and engage more with the alternative relationship story they would prefer.

Rather than resolving problem issues through an exploration of underlying interests (Fisher & Ury, 1981; Moore, 1996) in order to arrive at a relationship shift, the narrative approach aims to shift the relationship story onto a new footing so that the remaining issues between the disputants can be addressed from within a different narrative—ideally one that is more satisfying and invigorating than the conflict narrative.

Narrative mediation proceeds from the premise that persons are multi-storied rather than single-storied (White, 2007; Winslade & Monk, 2008). The same can be said for relationships. Any particular story of a relationship is only one of a selection of possible stories that can be told. The story that makes a conflict seem inevitable, justifiable, or at least understandable can best be understood as a narrative that has come to dominate, rather than as essential to the nature of the parties' relationship. If we are prepared to search for it, there usually exist, in the shadows of a conflict story, other stories of relationship that are being subordinated (White, 2007) by the dominance of the conflict story. The aim of narrative mediation is to rescue such subordinate stories from the oblivion to which they are consigned and to recuperate them in the lives of those who have been in conflict.

STEPS IN THE PROCESS OF NARRATIVE MEDIATION

1. As with other approaches, narrative mediation begins with listening to the conflict story. The job of the mediator is to listen in a way that facilitates the articulation of the conflict story, acknowledging each of the parties, asking questions to elicit the story, summarizing what has been heard,

and checking regularly for accuracy. It also involves the distinctively narrative skill of "double listening" (listening for both the problem story and the counter story). Early on, the counter story will usually be weak and not strongly represented. But it is implicitly present in people's hope for a different kind of conversation and in their very presence in the room.

2. The next stage of a narrative mediation process is to develop an externalizing conversation and to map the effects of the conflict. The externalized name for the conflict should encompass both parties' experience, rather than focus more on one person's experience at the expense of the other. Often it is enough to refer to the argument, the tension, or the situation. Whatever name is chosen should be decided in consultation with the parties, rather than out of the mediator's head. Mapping the effects of the problem should attend to the three dimensions of its length, breadth, and depth. *Length* refers to time ("How long has it been happening?"), *breadth* refers to the different domains of life that have been affected ("How far have its effects spread? How have you limited it from affecting other things? Besides yourselves, who else has been affected?"), and *depth* refers to the extent and severity of its impact ("How hard have its effects been? How badly are you affected?").

3. The third step in narrative mediation is to evaluate the conflict story and its effects and to establish a preference for something different. This is often a very brief step, taking less than a minute, but is often critical in a relationship re-authoring process. It involves the mediator inquiring into what the parties think of what the conflict story is doing and all of its effects. The disputants are invited to make a judgment, not of each other but of the story itself ("Is all this acceptable to you? Can you tolerate it? Or would you prefer things to be different? If so, what would you prefer?"). Whatever people say they would prefer is an opening into a counter story to the problem story.

4. The fourth step in narrative mediation is to expand upon the preferred relationship story. It is expanded by establishing its history ("When has what you would prefer happened in the past?") and its future ("What would things look like in the future if what you would prefer was happening?"). It is also expanded by being developed on the landscape of action ("Can you give me an example of what that would look like?") and on the landscape of meaning ("What is the significance of that action? What difference does it make?"). Parties who start to identify with this counter story can be asked to justify it ("Why do you prefer this? Does it fit better with your best intentions? How so?"). The counter story can also be strengthened by giving it a name that serves as a reference point for all the details mentioned in this story (for example, "civil conversation," "good atmosphere," "cooperation").

5. The final step in a narrative mediation is to invite people to negotiate what still needs to be agreed upon in the spirit of the counter story.

As in other approaches to such negotiations, options should be brainstormed without evaluation, and then later these options should be assessed for their potential to form elements of an agreement.

A CASE VIGNETTE

The process of narrative mediation can be outlined in the introduction as we have done above, but it does not come to life until embodied in a real situation. We shall now, therefore, include a story of a mediation that took place in a school. It is a mediation undertaken by a school counselor between two teenage boys who have been caught fighting.

Fighting between students at high schools is traditionally dealt with by punishing the protagonists. Punishment, however, often gives no guarantee that the conflict is resolved and often produces unwanted side effects (resentment toward authorities, alienation from schooling, threats of retribution, professional frustration, and so on). Mediation is an alternative action that can restore relationship and lead to a more lasting resolution of conflict without negative residual aftereffects.

The story happened in a New Zealand high school. The situation quickly escalated into a fight between two boys. After a referral to the school counselor, the two boys took part in a mediation conversation. Through this process, the two students redefined aspects of their identities to make it more likely that they might realize their hopes for success at school.

Mike Williams was the school counselor who mediated the conversation. The story is written from his perspective. The names of the boys have been changed to protect their anonymity. Both gave permission for this story to be published.

> *I deliberately left my office door open so that when the boys arrived I could greet them. When they arrived, I raised my eyebrows quickly in the Polynesian manner of greeting and motioned for them to sit down.*
>
> *"Hi, boys," I smiled. "You're not in trouble, but there is something we need to get sorted. I guess you were expecting this meeting?"*
>
> *"Yeah, the Deputy Principal told us you wanted to talk to us," the taller boy retorted.*
>
> *Both boys held their heads high in defiance. I smiled to myself as I thought how important it was for these two to protect their mana. (Mana is a Polynesian, and especially Maori, concept that signifies a status of being worthy of respect. One is partly born into it, and it can also grow in social contexts.)*
>
> *They sat on opposite sides of the room not looking at each other. There was tension and strain between the two.*
>
> *"You're right about meeting to talk," I explained, "but actually it wasn't my idea for me to talk to you. I would rather you talked to me. I heard you nearly had a fight."*
>
> *"Yeah," said the other boy, "I could have smashed him but I didn't."*
>
> *The boys were in no mood to discuss anything, but I persevered.*

"What I would like to hear is how it came to this. I have studied fights over the years in my job, and I would love to hear about this one," I said. "My guess is that both of you are surprised to be here in this room and that this fight just crept up on you and you weren't expecting it. Is that right?" They both nodded imperceptibly.

Externalizing Conversation

Here the mediator positions the parties in a grammatical shift through utilizing the narrative technique of externalizing. The conflict itself is objectified and spoken of as if it has designs on the two parties, rather than as something that originated in either of them. The mediator refers to the fight as something "that crept up on you." The deliberately non-blaming language allows some saving of face, rather than encouraging blame. The mediator rejects collaboration with either party (or with the school authorities) and seeks to privilege the boys' telling of the story and its uniqueness and size.

"When we have meetings like this," I continued, "I usually get people to talk one at a time and tell the story of what happened. Then we look for a solution to the problem and work out how to move forward. How does that sound?"

Silence.

"You're Joshua, and you're Jeremy, is that right?"

"Yes," they both said.

"Has there been some 'beef' between you two for a while?" I inquired.

"I hardly know him," Joshua said. "I didn't go to his intermediate school."

I looked at the two boys closely.

"Who would like to start?" I asked.

"Well, I came round the corner of B Block on Monday with my mates, and he looked at me," Jeremy said.

A look, I thought. It must have been more than that! But I kept my thoughts to myself.

"Then what happened?"

"I just kept walking and wondered if he wanted to fight. My mates said he looked like he wanted a fight, and they asked me if I was I going to smash him," Jeremy said.

"What did you think about them saying that?" I asked.

"Well, I wasn't sure if he wanted to fight, but they said he did," Jeremy replied.

"Then what?"

"I went up to him and collared him and asked him if he wanted a fight," Jeremy explained.

> *"What did he say?" I asked.*
> *"He said he didn't want to fight, but I was sure he was lying."*
> *"Were you?" I looked over at Joshua.*
> *"Nah," said Joshua. "I am not allowed to fight. I am a boxer."*
> *"How come you are not allowed to fight?" I asked.*
> *"Well, if I fight at school, I get stood down from my club," he said. "I have had 21 fights, 19 were K.O.'s and 2 were decisions," he said proudly.*
> *"What do those numbers mean?"*
> *"It means I have had 21 fights for my club and I won them all!"*
> *I noticed a small movement of surprise on Jeremy's face as he heard this.*
> *"I am sorry," I explained, "I have jumped ahead here. I haven't given you a chance to tell your story," I said to Joshua.*
> *"It's simple," Joshua said. "I was just sitting on the bench and these boys came round the corner and with the sun behind them. I thought I recognized Jeremy but he was hard to see in the sun and I kind of screwed up my eyes," he explained. "Yeah I looked at him, but not like he said."*
> *"Then what happened?" I asked curiously.*
> *"He came up to me with his boys and I stood up to meet him and he collared me. That's when the teacher came and broke it up. I didn't want to fight him. I am not allowed to fight."*

Double Listening

The mediator here has listened to the story from both parties. Like many conflict stories, it features a narrow range of positions (Winslade, 2005; Winslade & Monk, 2008), by which each person feels constrained. The mediator has been hearing the conflict story but at the same time keeping an ear out for openings to an alternative story, especially one that might work against violence. Joshua's last remark presents itself as an opening to such an alternative story. The mediator explores it further. Rather than inquiring further into the motives for fighting (which would risk making fighting seem more justified and inevitable), he deliberately shifts to asking about narrative elements that work in the opposite direction. He expresses curiosity about the parties' knowledge of what might make a difference, rather than speaking with authority and trying to convince the boys of the correctness of this voice.

> *"What held you back from fighting, apart from what your club said?"*
> *"My parents would be angry if I fight. I want to stay at school. And there's my girlfriend. She told me that if I fight at school, she's gonna dump me."*
> *I wondered about what these expectations meant for Joshua. "What are the rules about fighting, Joshua?"*
> *"Well," he began, "there are club rules . . . and . . . you get kicked out if you fight anywhere the club has not approved."*
> *"Any other rules about fighting?" I asked with curiosity. "School rules, maybe?"*
> *"Well I don't really care about school rules," he said with pride, "but yeah, you're not allowed to fight at school."*

"I heard you say there were some family rules," I suggested. His head lowered. "Yeah," he said.

"And your girlfriend has some rules too?"

"She doesn't like fighting."

"Could there be rules that adults and teachers don't know about?" I inquired nonchalantly. "Maybe kids' rules . . . ? One kid told me the other day that if someone asks you for a fight, you have to give it. Is that a kind of 'rule'?"

"Well, it's not really a rule," he retorted. "It's just something you have to do, but I don't buy it!"

Identifying Counter Stories

Joshua here articulates a range of knowledges of the reasons for nonviolence. Such knowledges do not fit with his participation in the fight, but a narrative mediator is less interested in narrative congruence than in opening up contrast between the conflict story and a possible alternative story. The latter was largely excluded from the initial stories told by each boy, but it has now been made possible to talk about. This has not happened by accident but because of a particular form of listening and inquiring.

"What do you want to do when you leave school?" I changed tack.

"I want to be an architect," Joshua said with pride.

"You'll have to stay away from fighting then," I joked.

I turned again to Jeremy. "Now that you've heard what Joshua has said, does that change anything?" I asked.

"Yeah, I found out he doesn't want to fight me, so it would be a boring fight, because he wouldn't fight back," he said.

"Are the rules the same for you as for Joshua?" I asked. "What would your parents or family say if they knew about this fighting?"

"I would be in trouble, if they knew, but I just got angry and my mates were saying he looked at me."

The counter story has been grown further by inquiry into Jeremy's knowledge of reasons to avoid fighting. Rather than emphasizing rules from the point of view of authority, the mediator seeks out more pragmatically effective rules: those subscribed to by the parties themselves. Jeremy, too, was able to reference family values that run counter to the violent expression of conflict. He was also able to offer a construction of fighting as having no point in the event that the fight would be a "boring fight."

I wondered how much both boys knew about the effects of anger. "How do guys like you manage their anger?" I asked.

"I joined boxing," Joshua offered, "and that really helped. I work out, and I don't let myself get angry. I need to think straight," Joshua continued.

"If a boy is able to manage anger well, how do you think it would help?" I wondered aloud. This hypothetical question inquires further into the boys' counter knowledge to the story of the problem.

> *"It would mean that I have a future. I want to be an architect," he reminded me.*
> *"What do you want to do when you leave school, Jeremy?" I asked.*
> *"Accountant," he said sheepishly.*
> *"What would happen to your future, if you got sidetracked by fighting?"*
> *He looked at the floor. "It wouldn't happen."*
> *The room went silent, and both boys were thinking deeply about what we were discussing. I looked up as if I had an idea, and I stretched my hands out in the air and described plaques on a building. "I can just see it now," I said excitedly. "Jeremy, Accountant, and Joshua, Architect!" They both smiled, and I knew we were making progress.*

The mediator here continues to practice externalizing by talking about first anger and then fighting as external forces that threaten both boys' dreams of a future. In the last question, he is doing a little mapping of the effects of the problem. In this case, the effects do not just exist in the present but also in an imagined future. We assume that it is more productive to explore such effects than to inquire into the causes of a conflict. Studying the causes of a conflict entrenches it further as inevitable, whereas studying its effects opens up more places where changes can be made. As this conversation develops, the two boys are steadily stepping out of the relational place that the conflict story has prescribed. They are now starting to speak from within a different narrative.

> *"Can you see how pressure from others can make us do things we might not want to do?" I asked, using externalizing language again to refer to pressure and separate it from what the two boys might "want to do."*
> *"I wonder if Joshua's boxing reputation was known to a few kids, and they wanted you to test him," I said, looking inquisitively at Jeremy. "I suppose you were going through a bit of a test yourself, Jeremy? I wonder what you can tell your mates now about Joshua."*
> *"I am going to tell them that he's all right and that we sorted it out with your help," he replied.*
> *"You two are doing the sorting out," I smiled. I didn't mind, however, if he used me to save face with his friends.*
> *"Let's see if we can capture all these ideas we have discovered," I said. "Let's make a chart so we can see what we have learned." On my whiteboard, I wrote down their ideas headed up with the following:*

> ### Brilliant Excuses to Resist Fighting
> - School/club/family rules
> - Future in danger of being wrecked
> - Girlfriend/brothers/dad don't want me to fight
> - Wouldn't be a proper fight

> "That's a good start," I said. "Can we turn that into an agreement?" I asked. They nodded cautiously. Under the bullet points, I wrote
>
> Contract Between Jeremy and Joshua, March 11, 2009

What was being recorded on the whiteboard were the meanings drawn from the counter narrative to the story of fighting. Each boy had contributed to this list, and it referred to concepts and experiences that had currency in their cultural world. It was not a list imposed on them from the school's perspective or from any professional expertise. It therefore stood a better chance of taking effect. Taking spoken words and rendering them in written form grants the words greater authority and status and allows them to reverberate longer in consciousness. Using the parlance of the protagonists honors the uniqueness of this particular conflict and its corresponding resolution. The two boys and the mediator were about to construct an entirely new relationship, with a storyline that had not existed before. The publication of the contract repudiated any reputation the boys may have had as "troublemakers" or "fighters" (Epston, 2008).

Negotiating Agreement

Now it was time to negotiate agreement about how to go forward. This negotiation is built upon the counter story of relationship that has already been established, rather than on the telling of the conflict story. Here the mediator judged that the talk about the reasons to resist fighting was strong enough to build some concrete actions upon it.

> "What have we decided to do about our 'beef' after this meeting?" I inquired. "Would you like to write one part of the deal each?"
>
> Joshua came first to the whiteboard and wrote, "We've sorted it out."
> Jeremy came up and added, "It's all good now."
> Then, without prompting, they signed their names, and before I had a chance to say anything, Joshua turned to Jeremy and said, "I am sorry I looked at you."
> I looked startled, as I wasn't expecting this, because Joshua wasn't the aggressor. Jeremy responded by saying, "I am sorry too. I shouldn't let other people peer-pressure me."
> They embraced and patted each other on the back and sat down smiling. I wanted to join in the hugs as well! I thanked them for their willingness to meet and sent them back to class.
> I heard from the Deputy Principal the next day that both boys had gone over to his office before returning to class and told him excitedly that "It was sorted." Both boys apologized and said they were sorry for giving him "grief"!

Re-storying Students' Identities

The denouement of this particular drama was actually very quick and easy. The boys had embraced an alternative story of relationship that featured "reasons to resist fighting" and had used it to take actions that would not have been predicted at the start of the conversation when they were both in the thrall of the conflict. The apologies had been volunteered, and the hugs appeared spontaneous. The idea of going to speak to the Deputy Principal and to restore relationship with him and with the school had also come from the boys themselves. Each of these actions was a plot development in the counter narrative. Telling the Deputy Principal that the conflict had been resolved enhanced the possibility that reputations of fighting might not be permanently assigned. Such counter stories constitute new stories of self-definition and require recognition within the school for their construction and maintenance (Lindemann Nelson, 2001).

Once such a narrative has taken root, it can continue to send out new shoots and, like a rhizome (Deleuze & Guattari, 1987), extend its coverage through sending down further roots in new territory. It would likely take root in the relationships with the bystanders to the original fight, for example. And both boys might need to speak to the story that "It's sorted" with their respective families, girlfriends, and boxing club trainers. The conflict that had sparked this story had created new relational spaces for both boys. The story of resolution and reconciliation needed also to spread beyond the walls of the counseling room. Friends of the two protagonists would not expect such a dramatic outcome and would be interested to know how it was achieved. Conflict stories do not exist only in the worlds of the major protagonists but are woven into the webs of relationship of which they are a part. So too must an alternative story (or a counter story) be woven into these same relationship webs.

Subverting the expected plot trajectory provides the young people with access to new forms of community. In Joshua's case, resisting the call to fight solidified his position in the school as someone with physical power who chose not to exert it. Jeremy, on the other hand, regraded himself as someone who had escaped the jaws of punishment by taking a mature approach and resisted the temptation to fight. As the wider school community recognized the identity shifts, it coauthored the description of these boys as morally competent young men. The more these boys acted as they were expected to, the more they fulfilled that plot.

SUMMARY

In this chapter, we have outlined a narrative approach to mediation that can be used by school administrators or counselors. It involves helping people in dispute to separate from identifying closely with a relationship story that is saturated with conflict and stepping into a counter story of relationship, one that features cooperation, understanding, and resolution. A key step in this process is the externalizing of the conflict and the identification of actions that do not fit with the ongoing escalation of the conflict. These elements of a counter story are then examined for their history and projected into a future.

QUESTIONS FOR REFLECTION

1. What stands out about the differences between a narrative approach to mediation and other mediation models?

2. Practice double listening to a television debate and noticing openings to a story of agreement, despite the dominant narrative of conflict.

3. How often, after a fight in a school, do adults pay attention to what the students involved can tell them about how not to get caught up in fighting?

4. In developing an externalizing conversation, what works best to externalize and what is less effective?

QUESTIONS FOR RESEARCH

1. Collect an archive of mediation stories in a school. How did they work? What did they achieve? How was their success evaluated? What can be learned from them?

2. Generate a case study of one use of mediation in a school conflict.

5

Peer Mediation

INTRODUCING PEER MEDIATION

In the last chapter, we discussed the practice of mediation by skilled adults. Now we want to advocate that these practices be entrusted to young people, and even children. In many schools, students trained to operate as peer mediators have operated effectively as peacemakers. They need training and guidance (the younger they are, the more guidance they will need), but adults also need to learn to trust that students can solve problems in their own ways. They are members of local communities of youth knowledge, to which adults have only partial access and marginal understanding. Often students are best placed to be aware of what is happening between other students and to help resolve such conflicts.

As educators and school leaders, our job is to provide them with opportunities and support. One function of schools is to develop citizens for a democracy in which leadership is shared among many. If this does not involve learning how to facilitate conversations about differences between people, then it is hard to imagine what could be more important. The world of the future is likely to demand such skills in even greater quantities than that of the present. What better leadership training for students for such a future than learning how to deal with conflict!

When students are trained in these skills, they cannot help but let them flow into the fabric of the school. They begin to "live that way." They start to view relationships through different lenses and to act in ways that express their new role. They become agents of change in the school no matter what their age and affect the "tone" of the school as they take a stand against bullying and relational aggression. They may even challenge the ways that adults sometimes speak to children!

If you have ever had the experience of talking with student peer mediators about their enthusiasm for conflict resolution, then you will know how easy it is to be inspired by their energy and drive. It is hard to find any better source of hope for the future than to listen to what such groups of young people have to say. Many high school students are capable of understanding quite complex concepts in conflict resolution and of practicing them in ways that many teachers would be proud of. They can often cut to the chase in conflict situations more quickly than adults. A consistent theme among students who become peer mediators is that they learn more about interpersonal skills for themselves than they ever offer to other students through the services they perform. This is not the kind of learning that necessarily helps them pass school tests, but it is definitely of the kind that helps them live their lives.

In this chapter, we describe a process developed for high school students and using language appropriate to that age. The process outlined below could, however, be used to develop a training program for children as young as fourth grade. Without being condescending, scripts and dialogues that younger children themselves might use could be written for them. Once they become skilled and more confident, they need not rely on the scripts. A laminated card with question prompts or key words could provide the support that younger children require as they grow in this role.

For a theoretical justification for the work of peer mediators, we can turn to the work of Lev Vygostky (1978, 1986). Vygotsky showed the value of students learning from peers who were closer to them in the learning process than adults. The term he coined was the "zone of proximal development," which he defined as

> the distance between the actual developmental level as determined by independent problem solving and the level of potential development as determined through problem solving under adult guidance or in collaboration with more capable peers. (1978, p. 86)

In the zone of proximal development, students can be assisted to move toward mastering a new skill with the assistance of someone who is close to their level of learning but slightly ahead of them. The slightly advanced learner can help "scaffold" the learning. Vygotsky's ideas have in recent decades received much attention in educational psychology and have greatly benefited fields such as reading. They are equally applicable in the context of learning relational skills.

In this chapter, we shall focus mainly on the process of training peer mediators rather than on the details of setting up a peer mediation program. The shaping of such a program needs to be embedded in the culture of a particular school, and we do not want to prescribe it too precisely for fear of insisting on something that works in one context but not in another. What we *can* do is specify some questions that may need to be resolved along the way. We list these here as questions to be answered—see Box 5.1.

BOX 5.1
ISSUES TO BE RESOLVED IN ESTABLISHING
A PEER MEDIATION SERVICE IN A SCHOOL

1. How will peer mediators be chosen? Through what kind of process will they apply? What kind of screening will be used? Who will be ruled out? (Note that many have found that students who have been involved in conflicts themselves often make good mediators.)

2. How will the peer mediators be trained? Over what period of time? As part of the school curriculum and timetable or as an extracurricular activity?

3. How will the peer mediation service receive referrals? How will mediators be assigned? How will mediators be rostered?

4. What resources will be allocated to the peer mediation program? Rooms? Budget? Forms? Training resources? Backup supervision? Secretarial help?

5. Will mediations happen during school lesson time or only at lunchtime and before or after school?

6. How will the service be publicized to other students and teachers?

7. How will conflicts involving a teacher and a student be handled?

8. How will peer mediators be identified in their role around the school? Badges? Clipboards? T-shirts? Certificates awarded by the principal?

9. How will the work of peer mediators be acknowledged (including on a student's record of achievement)?

10. How will mediation and conflict resolution ideals be spread throughout the culture of the school?

(Continued)

(Continued)

11. How will the peer mediation approach be sustained?

12. How can peer mediation fit within the culture of the school?

13. How can we ensure that the confidentiality of the mediation process is respected by both students and staff?

14. Who will be responsible for coordinating the program, and how will continuity be provided for?

Once a group of peer mediators has been trained, they can be set to a range of conflict resolution functions. They need not wait until conflicts present themselves neatly packaged as suitable for mediation. They can be engaged in a range of strategies to promote peaceful relations in the school. Box 5.2 lists some tasks that can be delegated to them.

BOX 5.2
LIST OF PEACE-BUILDING FUNCTIONS
IN WHICH PEER MEDIATORS CAN ENGAGE

1. Identifying different groups in the school and setting up dialogues between them.

2. Developing anti-bullying campaigns.

3. Watching for cyber bullying among students and acting to defuse it.

4. Participating as role players in guidance lessons (see Chapter 10).

5. Organizing a peace week and planning events, such as face painting and wearing hats and wigs.

6. Designing a campaign to counter prejudice toward LGBT students.

7. Inserting a daily peace quote in the daily school news bulletin.

8. Listening to the discourse in schools that is producing conflict and bringing that discourse to light.

9. Monitoring sexual violation at school dances.

10. Launching a consciousness-raising campaign against date rape.

11. Mentoring students in trouble with teachers on a regular basis.

12. Regularly reporting to the school community in a newsletter.

13. Organizing and carrying out fundraising activities.

14. Advertising on the school radio station.

15. Producing a video or DVD.

16. Inviting the local newspaper to do a feature article.

17. Publishing an article in an academic journal.

18. Creating a mission statement for peace and peer mediation in English classes, creating banners in art classes, and writing music or raps in music classes.

19. Having a school social event sponsored by the peer mediation program.

20. Demonstrating conflict resolution processes to parents at parent evenings.

21. Meeting school evaluators when they do regular school audits.

22. Making origami cranes as symbols of peace.

THE PROCESS OF MEDIATION

In order for the process of mediation to be learned by students, it needs to be simplified a little. Students also need to have a standard step-by-step process to rely on, especially when they are beginning to practice mediation. We have, therefore, devised a template of simplified guidelines for mediators that can be used by beginners. As students gain more practice, they can put it to one side and be more flexible. This set of guidelines is based on the same narrative principles that pervade this book. It is summarized as a checklist in Box 5.3.

BOX 5.3
GUIDELINES FOR PEER MEDIATORS

The Mediation Process

1. Setting up	Arrange chairs to suit.
	Open window if needed.
	Clear table of "junk."

(Continued)

(Continued)

2. Introduction and Ground Rules	Welcome students and tell them where to sit.
	Introduce yourself.
	Outline what is going to happen.
	Give them guidelines for behavior.
	Remind them of confidentiality.
3. Storytelling Phase	Use active listening skills to hear each student.
	Use open-ended questions.
	Externalize the conflict story.
	Map the effects of the conflict.
	Summarize.
4. Finding Solutions	Ask whether parties want conflict to continue or prefer something different.
	Ask what they would prefer.
	List all possible options for resolution.
	Explore each one: Feasibility? Consequences?
5. The Agreement	Check that both parties agree on action.
	Get action started.
	Sum up.
	Write down agreed-upon options and get both students to sign.
	Organize follow-up.
6. Closure	Hand in copy of agreement.
	Debrief with school counselor.

Stage 1: Setting Up

It is best for student mediators to work in pairs. Roles between the two should be clearly assigned. For example, one student should be designated to take careful notes on what is said, while the other leads the conversation. Roles can then be switched at some point during the conversation.

Finding a suitable room that is free from interruption is the first task. Then it is necessary to set the room up, arrange the chairs, close blinds or curtains for privacy, and decide where the mediators will sit (usually between the parties) and where the students in dispute will sit.

Stage 2: Introduction and Ground Rules

The first task is to welcome everyone to the meeting in a friendly but businesslike manner. Remember that people in conflict may be anxious about being in the same room with each other, so avoid sounding too chatty and happy or you might put them off the process quickly. Introductions come next. Introduce yourselves, and make sure you have learned the parties' names correctly and spelled them accurately on the form. Introduce the mediation process so the parties know what to expect, and establish guidelines for the conversation so that everyone feels safe and comfortable enough to speak.

What to say:

Welcome. I'm Vanessa and this is Michael. If it's acceptable to you, we will be your mediators. Is that okay?

That's good. Thanks for coming. Here is what will happen. You will both get a chance to tell your stories and explain how you have been affected by what's happened. Then we will see if we can come to an agreement about how we can solve this problem so that it doesn't come back again.

Is that okay?

Good. In order for this mediation to work, we need to agree on some rules. Would you both please be willing to agree to

- Listen to each other's point of view without interrupting?
- Work out how to solve the problem?
- Avoid name-calling, insults, arguing, or giving dirty looks?
- Be honest and tell the truth?
- Speak to us first before speaking to each other?

Are these rules acceptable to you?
As mediators, we will

- Not tell you what to do.
- Not take sides.
- Help you solve the problem yourselves.
- Not tell anybody anything you share with us unless it is illegal, or could be harmful to you or someone else.

Is that okay?
Good. Thank you.

Stage 3: Storytelling

Now it is time to hear the story of what happened. There will be at least two versions of this story. Both may seem plausible, and it is not the mediator's job to decide which one is right. The motto to bear in mind is, *The person is not the problem; the problem is the problem.*

Listen for the key words used by each person and reflect these back. This is active listening. Also practice double listening and hear both the problem story and each person's desire for something different. Ask questions to explore what each person was thinking as the conflict developed. Ask them too about what they were assuming. After each person has spoken, summarize what happened.

Then it is time to externalize the conflict story. Ask the two parties to give it a name and see if they can agree on this name. It should be a name for the situation between them, not one that names either person as the problem.

Once a name for the conflict story has been agreed on, it is now time to map the effects of the conflict on each of the parties and on other people around them. This is achieved by taking the externalized name for the problem and asking, "How has the 'tension' affected you both?" Ask this question several times until you have heard and acknowledged the effects of the conflict. Continue to use active listening during this conversation.

What to say:

> *This mediation will focus on only what has happened between you, Deirdre, and you, Dion. We will discuss what harm has been done by this conflict and what must be done to put things right again.*
>
> *To help us all understand the harm done and the effects of the conflict, we will ask you some questions that may be hard to answer, but it's important to ask them so that we can find the best solutions to the problem.*
>
> *Deirdre, would you start? From your point of view, what happened?*
> *What were you thinking at the time?*
> *What assumptions led you to become part of this conflict?*
> *What have you thought about since it happened?*
> *Okay, here is a summary of what you have said.*
> *Dion, can I ask you the same questions I asked Deirdre? From your point of view, what happened?*
> *What were you thinking at the time?*
> *What assumptions did you make that led you to become part of this conflict?*
> *What have you thought about since it happened?*
> *Okay, here is a summary of what you have said.*

After both students have told their stories and agreed with the retelling of them by the mediator, ask the following:

> *Is there anything else either of you would like to add?*
>
> *Now can we agree on a name to call this conflict? If we were to describe the situation and give it a name, what would we call it? For instance, is it an argument? A tension? A row? A fight? A nasty development? Or what?*
>
> *Okay, so we are agreed that we will call it a [tension]. Now let us explore what effect this tension has been having on you both.*

What other effects has it had?
How does it get you feeling? Acting? Speaking to each other?
What has been the worst part of its effects?
Does it get you to do things against your better judgment? If so, what?
How has it affected other people?
    Thank you. Here is a summary of the effects of the tension you have told us about.

Stage 4: Finding Solutions

By this point, both parties are likely ready to step into, or at least entertain, an alternative story. To test this out, ask them what they think of the effects of the conflict as just acknowledged. Ask them to make a judgment, not about the other person, but about the problem. Is it okay with them for the conflict to be doing all these things? Can they tolerate it continuing, or would they prefer something different? You can even ask what would happen if it kept on getting worse.

If they would prefer something different, then ask them to describe what they would prefer. You might get answers such as that they would like things to be peaceful. Some might suggest that they do not want to be close friends but at least do not want to be enemies. Once a statement like this has been made and acknowledged by both parties, it is time to move to sorting out an agreement. Sometimes, however, a conflict can be dissolved without any need for an agreement, but this is not always the case. Mediators should be prepared for the negotiation of an agreement, in case it is needed.

The first stage in sorting out an agreement is to brainstorm a list of options to include in a resolution. Judgment should be suspended while this list is being developed. All ideas should be included, even some that appear off the wall. In this way, creativity becomes part of the process.

The next step is to go through all of the options on the list and to ask the parties to weigh each idea with regard to its feasibility and its possible consequences.

What to say:

Dion and Deirdre, what do you think of the tension having these effects? Is it okay with you? Could you tolerate it continuing like this, or even getting worse? Or would you prefer something different?
    So what exactly would you prefer? How would things be between you if they were more like what you would prefer? What would you like to see happen from this mediation to get to that point? What can you offer to do to help this happen?

The mediator summarizes their responses.

We will list all the ideas you can think of that might solve this problem. Please don't judge any of these ideas as good or bad for now. Let's just list them first.

> *Now that we have a list of possible solutions, let's go through each one and have you say what you think of it. Will it work? What would be the consequences of agreeing to do that?*

The mediator summarizes.

Stage 5: The Agreement

The next step is to negotiate agreement. If the earlier stages have gone well, this can happen quite quickly. Write down what has been agreed upon. It is important to record details as accurately as possible in the parties' own words. Once the agreement has been written, read it back to the parties and ask if they are willing to sign it.
What to say:

> *What might you both now agree on to reduce the effects of the tension and make peace possible? What can you offer each other? What do you want the other person to agree to?*
> *Say that again slowly so we can write it down.*
> *Okay. This is what you have said that you will agree to.*

The mediator reads out loud the terms of agreement.

> *Is that all correct? Did we leave anything out?*
> *So are you now both willing to sign this agreement?*
> *Good. Thank you.*

Stage 6: Closure

It remains for the mediators to both sign the agreement and set a date to review how the agreement has been adhered to. Then the agreement is passed to the school counselor to keep on file. The parties may be offered a copy of the agreement.
Now that the work of the mediation is complete, it is possible for some acknowledgment of what has been achieved to take place. This should be tempered by the fact that the agreement is, as yet, just words on paper and has still to be enacted in daily life. The parties can, nevertheless, be thanked for their willingness to join in a constructive conversation and for their willingness to reach agreement. They may not be completely happy with each other or want to be close friends, so do not expect too much. They can, however, be asked whether they are happy with how the conversation went. To acknowledge this can help strengthen the agreement that was reached.
What to say:

> *Just so you know, we will now sign and date this agreement ourselves. Then we will give it to Mr. Williams, the school counselor. He will keep it on file, so if there is any dispute, we can all refer back to it. Would you like a copy too?*

> *Thanks for working hard to resolve this conflict. The agreement you've reached should go a long way to repair the harm that has been done by the conflict. Can we all meet here again in 2 weeks to check that everything is working out? To prevent rumors from dragging you back into the tension, please tell your friends that the conflict has been resolved.*
>
> *Congratulations! We are impressed with what you have done. Are you pleased too?*

PEER MEDIATION TRAINING

There is a range of training manuals that are used in schools for peer mediation training. Few, if any, of these contain the narrative emphasis that has been demonstrated above. Specifically, this emphasis is about using externalizing language to name the conflict, mapping the effects of the conflict, inviting the parties to judge the effects of the conflict, and inviting them to state a preference for an alternative story. All this happens as a prelude to negotiating agreement, and usually it leads to an easy and smooth negotiation process. It also potentially produces a relational shift that is palpable and does as much as any agreement reached to undermine the conflict story and open up possibilities for a counter story.

Since this process emphasis is not widely known, we want to include in this chapter an outline of a training program that can prepare students to operate in this way. It is specifically aimed at high school students. In addition to coaching students in the use of the process outlined above, this training program is based on what have been called the hallmarks of narrative mediation (Winslade & Monk, 2008, p. 3). These hallmarks are as follows:

1. Assume that people live their lives through their stories.
2. Avoid essentialist assumptions.
3. Engage in double listening.
4. Build an externalizing conversation.
5. Identify openings to an alternative story.
6. Re-author the relationship story.
7. Document progress.

Although these key ideas were not originally intended for mediation training in high school settings, we have found that, with the right kind of explanation, students are capable of taking up these ideas and applying them in mediation meetings with fellow students. At one high school, these key ideas were distilled and taught to a group of selected students over a 5-week period during their lunch hour.

Session 1

The first session of the training concentrates on these two hallmarks:

- Assume that people live their lives through their stories.
- Avoid essentialist assumptions.

A narrative approach not only values the telling of stories as remembered descriptions of events but also sees stories as constructing the ongoing narrative of a person's life.

The key ideas to be covered in this session are listed in Box 5.4.

BOX 5.4
NARRATIVE MEDIATION TRAINING:
KEY CONCEPTS FOR SESSION 1

Assume that people live their lives through their stories.

- Stories are not just reports. They shape our thinking and therefore shape our reality.
- When we tell a story, we create a reality.
- We are all multi-storied.
- No single description encompasses our lives or an event in relationships between people.
- Different stories are not equal. Some are stronger than others.
- There are always stories that have not yet been told.
- Every story is a selection from all possible plot elements and arrangement of this selection in a particular order.

Avoid essentialist thinking about persons.
Essentialist thinking assumes

- That people are driven by a core essence inside themselves that is more or less stable.
- That how a person comes across is because of some internal personality trait or fixed label of that person: for example, "She's an angry person," or "She's a victim type," or "He's a bully."
- That the complexity of life can be summed up in a single description.
- That problems between people are caused by something wrong (a deficit) inside one or both parties.

Instead of thinking of people in terms of labels that sum up in a glib way what is wrong with a person, mediators are encouraged to understand labels as products of stories. They are like a reputation that may or may not be earned. The important thing is that it is always possible to think outside the box with regard to any label or any story about a person. None of them is essential. People are always more complex than any story that is told about them. Box 5.5 contains an activity designed to help learn these concepts.

BOX 5.5
ACTIVITY 1: STORYTELLING

1. Tell each other a brief story of an experience of a conflict. Listen to the other person without interruption or comment.

2. Switch roles and repeat number 1. The listener becomes the speaker, and the speaker becomes the listener.

3. Summarize the main points you heard the other person say. Begin your retelling with the phrase, "I heard a story about..." Where was the story set? Who were the people? What roles did they play? What was the driving force behind the conflict?

4. Repeat the exercise, and tell the story from another person's perspective.

5. Discuss what was hard or easy about doing this exercise. What else did you notice about the person telling the story? About yourself listening to the story?

Activity 2: Avoid Essentialist Assumptions

1. Think of a label that has been given to you, positive or negative. Talk with a partner about how you got that label and what evidence there was for it. Think of a positive version of the label, and discuss which you prefer and why—for example, consider "stubborn" as "single-minded" or "focused."

2. What effects did that label have on you?

3. Did you accept the label or resist it? Why? How?

4. Think of a label that you may at some time have given to another person. Does this label sum up all that could be said about that person?

Session 2: Double Listening

The key concepts covered in this session are as follows:

- Double listening
- Alternative story
- Counter story

Double listening involves listening to the story with one ear and listening for alternative or counter stories with the other ear. An *alternative story* is a story of relationship that does not fit with the story of a conflict. Another term for this is a *counter story.* It means the same thing but emphasizes the way in which one story can work against a problem story. For example, a story of cooperation might be a counter story for a story of ongoing argument. To count as a story, it has to have a series of plot events, some characters, some themes, and a context in which it takes place.

Double listening involves listening to the problem story and also listening for contradictions, gaps in the story, or glimmers of hope. It means listening for examples of difference from the dominant story. It means listening to understand what it is like to be the person caught up in the dispute. Listen with the intention of supporting the person to figure out what to do. Listen as a researcher who wants to know more, not as a judge or juror.

Remember that simply by seeking mediation, students are expressing hope that things could be different. Hunt for this hope and ask about it. There is always a flipside of what they are saying. Every time someone says what he or she is not happy about, there is a flipside of what the person would prefer. Listen for and ask about the ways that the conflict story has distorted and wrecked the relationship the students would prefer to have with each other. Box 5.6 contains an exercise that can be used to practice the skill of double listening.

BOX 5.6
ACTIVITY: ENGAGE IN DOUBLE LISTENING

1. Revisit the story from last week with your partner.

2. Identify where there was a difference between what was being said and what was preferred.

3. See if you can identify any expressed hopes for things to be different.

4. Listen for what is being left out of the story.

5. Listen for pieces of information that are not considered important.

6. Listen for intentions to make things better.

Session 3: Build an Externalizing Conversation

The key concepts covered in this session are as follows:

- Externalizing the problem
- Mapping the effects of the problem

"Externalizing the problem" refers to a particular form of language use in which a conflict is talked about as if it were a third party in a dispute. It is personified and spoken about as separate from the individuals who are central to the dispute. "Mapping the effects of the problem" refers to a line of inquiry in which the externalized name of the conflict is used repeatedly, and the participants are asked about how it has affected them, individually or collectively. An actual map or diagram may sometimes be used.

Narrative mediation assumes that *the person is not the problem; the problem is the problem.* In situations of conflict, it is common for people to see each other as a bad person or an angry person, and there are many other negative labels that people can insert into the last sentence—for example, *stubborn, difficult, crazy, hypocritical, lying, violent,* and so on. In each case, it is common for people to say that the other person *is* this way. In other words, being that way is an aspect of the person's *nature.* If something is part of your nature, you must have been born that way and cannot really change it. At the same time, the person making the statement gives herself (and anyone else willing to listen) a sealed-off explanation for the causes of the conflict that cannot be easily challenged or proved wrong. One unfortunate side effect is that people can easily conclude that nothing can be done to change anything.

We use the term *externalizing conversations* as a way of speaking about a problem in a new and different way. It means speaking about a problem as separate from or outside the person. The origins of conflict might thus be said to lie *between* people rather than *inside* either individual. Speaking of problems in such a way means that there is no need to try to change a person's personality. Instead, the anger, pain, and suffering is attributed to the conflict itself. This form of language invites everyone to see the conflict as a third party with a life of its own.

Externalizing conversations focus attention more on *the effects of a conflict, rather than on its causes,* and allow people to consider whether or not they like those effects. Externalizing bypasses the assigning of blame or shame onto a person and makes way for an alternative story of solutions to emerge. Usually, the best externalized name for the problem is something simple, such as *the conflict, the argument, the tension, the situation,* or whatever fits the circumstances. The mediator can also ask the parties to come up with a name that they can both agree on.

If they do agree on a name, the mediator should continue to use this name. The next step in the process is to map the effects of the problem. The effects of the problem can be explored with regard to people's thoughts and feelings, relationships, school studies, physical difficulties (for example, headaches, sick feelings, lack of sleep), and any other domains of life. They can also be explored with regard to the past, present, and future. Box 5.7 contains an activity to help practice externalizing. The exercise on interviewing the problem in Chapter 10 is also useful for practicing the use of externalizing language.

BOX 5.7
ACTIVITY: EXTERNALIZING
THE PROBLEM AND MAPPING THE EFFECTS

1. With a conversation partner, briefly tell another recent story of a small conflict.

2. Remember to listen carefully to the story.

3. Together, think of a name for the problem. It might be a dispute, a fight, or a situation, for example. Think of how you might say, "It's a story of . . ." You might say, "What might we call this thing you are up against? Is it an argument? A fight? Tension? What would you call it?"

4. If you can't come up with a name, don't worry. Call it "it."

5. Map the effects of the conflict by asking the following:
   (a) How long has it been around?
   (b) How is it affecting you?
   (c) How does it get you to feel, think, and speak?
   (d) What is it talking you into?
   (e) Are there other areas of your life where it is having an effect? Where and how?
   (f) What might happen if it doesn't stop?
   (g) What would you prefer to happen?

Session 4: Identify Openings to an Alternative Story

The key concepts covered in this session are as follows:

- Alternative story
- Counter story
- Unique outcome

A *unique outcome* is an event or a statement that would not fit with the conflict story. It can be used as an opening to the development of a counter story.

The next step is to find such an opening. The story of conflict is one of many stories that can be told about a relationship. It always leaves out some events and selects in only those elements that suit the story being told. There are, however, always other stories that can be told about this relationship. You can look behind the scenes for earlier moments of cooperation, respect, and friendship. These are unique outcomes. Inquiring about them helps them grow the properties of a story (plot, character, themes, setting). Box 5.8 contains some questions that help identify unique outcomes and develop the counter or alternative story.

BOX 5.8
STARTING POINTS FOR A COUNTER STORY

1. Ask the parties if they like what this conflict is doing to them and their relationships. Why not? Then ask how they would prefer things to be.

2. Look for examples of events that were not part of the conflict story. Use double listening to notice these moments and inquire into them. For example, "William, you said you were both on the same football team and you had a good season. Does this mean that you have worked together as part of a team? How did you do that?"

3. Explore the opposite of a statement to uncover values that lie behind the conflict. For example, if someone says, "He is so aggressive. I don't think he should be like that at school," you could ask, "What kind of relationship would be best in a school? What experience have you had where peace rules at school?"

4. Ask directly for times when the conflict was not present. You could say, "It sounds like it was not always like this. Have there been times when you have been able to talk to each other?"

5. Ask about others in their family that the students look up to who are good at resolving conflict. Ask how that person would deal with such a problem and what he or she would say about it.

6. Ask for someone at the meeting who is not affected by the problem and solicit her advice on how to proceed. If nobody is unaffected, you could still ask hypothetically, "If you weren't affected by this conflict, what solutions could work?"

7. Ask if there are any ideas that anybody might have had but not tried yet. Ask whether they have been wishing they could do something but haven't yet acted on that wish.

There are many ways to open a counter story. Which one you choose depends on what has already been talked about. Double listening earlier on often gives you a clue. Just as it takes time for a conflict story to grow, it may take time and persistence to "grow" an alternative story. The mediator makes links between any positive moments, just as negative experiences became linked in the conflict story.

The mediator might say, "Since you both don't want to keep this conflict going because of the effect it is having on your learning, what suggestions could you make about cooperation and getting along?"

Or, "So, you are sick of this conflict and you don't want to get pushed into some action you will regret? You have been friends in the past, so how could you solve this problem?"

Or, "We understand that you don't want a bad reputation and you don't want your parents involved. What needs to happen to revive the spirit of friendship between you?"

Box 5.9 contains an activity designed to practice this part of the mediation process.

BOX 5.9
ACTIVITY: NEGOTIATING RESOLUTION

1. Role-play another conflict story and briefly map the effects of the conflict (for 5 minutes only).

2. Now choose three of the questions in Box 5.8 that seem most relevant to this situation.

3. Ask each of these questions, adapting them to fit the story as it has been told.

4. Summarize the responses given.

5. Ask both parties to suggest options for solving the problem that fit with their preference for something different. List these suggestions.

6. Go through each item on the list and ask (a) how feasible it is and (b) what its consequences might be.

Session 5: Writing the Agreement and Documenting Progress

It is now time to ask what the parties are prepared to agree on to make a difference to the conflict. They can answer this either by requesting things from each other or by offering things to each other.

Care should be taken to write down exactly what each person offers. Writing these things down gives greater permanence to agreements. Purely verbal agreements can fade over time. Also, a stronger commitment to maintaining new pathways can be gained by recording what preferred relationships will "look like" in the future. In order to write up an agreement accurately, it is important for mediators to take notes during the mediation, which can later be referred back to.

The final document should contain a brief description of what happened. It should be carefully written in externalizing language, and it should document what was agreed to. Box 5.10 contains a sample mediation agreement document. The headings can be used to develop a standard form for use by a mediation team.

BOX 5.10
MEDIATION AGREEMENT

What Happened?

- A fight happened on the soccer field between Jason and Jarrard. Punches were thrown, and teachers separated the two boys. Many other students saw the fight and were encouraging them to keep going. There was talk about gossiping and back-stabbing as the reason for the fight.

Who Was Involved?

- Jason and Jarrard. The people who were friends of the two boys were George, Michaela, Jose, and Moshe. They were all at the fight.

What Was the Effect?

What effect did this fight have on each of the persons involved?

- Jason and Jarrard were yelling and swearing at each other. That drew heaps of people onto the field. They felt angry and mad at being put into this fight by others.

What effect did the fight have on other people?

- Students have been texting others outside of school to come down after school to fight. Some students filmed the fight. People have taken sides and are fired up.

What Needs to Happen to Repair the Harm Done?

List the agreements.

- Jason and Jarrard will apologize for fighting each other, shake hands, and make peace.
- Both boys will write a letter to the principal and to the teacher who broke up the fight, apologizing for fighting and asking what else is required by them.
- Both boys will speak to an assembly to apologize to the whole school for fighting and express remorse for the effects on the school.
- Both boys will state on their Facebook pages that the fight has finished and there are no more actions they want anyone else to take.
- Both boys will text four people each and tell them the fight is over and not to come down.
- The principal will inform the parents about the fight and how it has been resolved.

Signatures of All Parties

Date of Agreement

What has happened in order for this document to be written? First, let us notice what the fight meant. Rather than an opportunity to sort things out, a fight represents an opportunity to rekindle a "beef," or extend a beef, or continue a beef with another person. It is usually not the end of a story but an elaboration of a storyline that will persist for some distance yet, one that features alliances and paybacks and saving face. The only way to bring this storyline to an end is to grow a new relationship between those caught up in the fight and those affected by the fight. For this reason, mediation is about more than reaching agreements or doing deals. It is in the end about re-storying relationships.

SUMMARY

This chapter has described a step-by-step process for narrative mediation between peers. It is a blueprint for the mediation process that is designed for students but can work for adults as well. We have tried to make it accessible, at the risk of making it too formulaic. Creative people will change and develop it, even in the process of copying it. Our hope too is that school counselors who want to teach students to do this work will practice it themselves. A substantial part of the work of a school counselor revolves around dealing with conflict in some form or another. Therefore, perhaps we have described how a school counselor could use narrative mediation even before students are exposed to it!

QUESTIONS FOR REFLECTION

1. How might this process be simplified further for middle school and elementary school mediators?

2. How might morale be sustained in a peer mediation team?

QUESTIONS FOR RESEARCH

1. How might the work of a peer mediation team be evaluated?

2. How can the effect of a peer mediation team on school climate be studied?

3. Collect an archive of stories of peer mediation work in a school.

6

Restorative Conferencing

THE PROBLEM WITH PUNISHMENT FOR DISCIPLINARY OFFENSES

When a student commits a serious disciplinary offense, it is common, especially under the regime of "zero tolerance," for the offender to be isolated from the context in which the offense occurred and then suspended permanently from the school. Such action is often framed as strong leadership by the school administration and justified as protective of the majority of the school community by getting rid of the "few" dangerous elements. The problem with this logic is that often the strong action succeeds, not in reducing violence in the school, but in shifting it out into the community, from where it returns to the school in a later manifestation.

Students who are expelled are also often launched into a "career" that ends up in the pipeline to prison. Suspension does nothing much to interrupt that trajectory and often propels it forward. Nor do the victims of the offense usually receive anything that might redress the harm done to them. At best, as in the criminal justice system, they are called upon to be witnesses who can aid the school authorities to show, not so much leadership, as power.

Our concern in such circumstances is that little in the way of learning has taken place. Neither the offender nor the victim gets to examine what led to the offense. Neither is asked to address the breach in relationship established by the offense. Damage done to people and property is not put right, at least not by the offender. What is created in the end is a split community in which the majority are taught to fear and protect themselves against the minority. It is out of a desire to do better than this that the restorative conferencing process was developed.

THE IDEA OF RESTORATIVE JUSTICE

A strong movement has gathered momentum in many parts of the world under the banner of "restorative justice." It includes a range of innovative conflict resolution practices that have been springing up in the domains of youth justice, adult criminal justice, community policing, social work practice, and schools. A leading figure in the articulation of the idea behind these practices is Howard Zehr (1990, 2002). What is distinctive about a restorative approach is the emphasis on understanding offending from a relational perspective. Zehr contrasts "restorative justice" with what he calls "retributive justice" (the dominant framework in most justice systems). *Retributive justice* aims to restore the authority of the state (or the school administration) after an offense has compromised that authority. The usual approach is to mete out punishment. By contrast, *restorative justice* invites us to view any offense first as an offense against other persons. It causes harm to others. It breaches relationship. It damages community. It cannot, therefore, be adequately addressed without attempting to redress the harm done to relationships and communities.

Legal systems have seldom offered victims of crime much other than the minor satisfaction of seeing offenders punished. Victims often receive little, if any, compensation for what they have lost, or emotional recognition for their humiliation, or satisfactory reassurance for their ongoing fears of being the target for further offending. Instead, they are left with a bitter taste when offenders plead not guilty in court and show little remorse. Schools are not much different. Victims can be left with a similar bitter taste when offenders are punished by school authorities and returned back to class to face their victims, who are sitting with the very real fear of retaliation.

By contrast, a restorative process concentrates on addressing the harm created by an offense. The voice of the victim of an offense is given a prominent hearing, and an offender is invited to set right the damage done. The restorative aspect should be carefully distinguished from an emphasis on rehabilitation. The difference is that offenders are required to take up responsibility toward victims, rather than just to work to change themselves. No excuses are made or sympathy sought for the difficult life circumstances that may justify the offending. A United Nations handbook defines restorative justice in this way:

> Restorative justice refers to a process for resolving crime by focusing on redressing the harm done to the victims, holding offenders accountable for their actions and, often also, engaging the community in the resolution of that conflict. (Dandurand & Griffiths, 2006, p. 6)

In this chapter, we shall explain a process for conducting a restorative conference in a school context. For a full account of the international movement to introduce restorative practices in community and school settings and for a summary of the highly promising research on effectiveness, readers are referred to Winslade and Monk (2008). There are different approaches to restorative conferencing, each of which differs in small but important ways. Here we shall concentrate on the approach that builds on a consistent narrative perspective. It can be read about in full in a practice-oriented monograph produced by the Restorative Practices Development Team (2004) at the University of Waikato. But first let us outline some principles on which this practice is founded.

PRINCIPLES OF A RESTORATIVE CONFERENCE

Build a Community of Care

A starting principle is the idea that any problem has around it a community of people who care about what happens or have a stake in the issue. The aim of a restorative conference is to bring together this community of care and to knit any resolution process into that community. It is an inclusive process, rather than one that isolates offenders and separates them out from the rest of the community. Suspension or expulsion from the school, by contrast, both work to separate the offender from community participation. At the same time, the process poses quite seriously the question, "Just what needs to happen in order for offenders to remain in community with persons they have done harm to?" The offender is offered the chance to be re-included in the school community, on the basis of her efforts to address the effects of the offense.

A school community that takes this stance should not be mistaken for being soft and overlooking the seriousness of offenses. On the contrary, this stance is more demanding of responsibility as a condition of community membership than the usual versions of "zero tolerance." We would argue that schools that take this approach are more socially responsible than those who simply exclude offenders and effectively pass problems on to other institutions, expecting them to hold an offender significantly accountable. The distinction lies in being effective and responsible, rather than being simply morally righteous.

There is often an experience of shame that is concomitant with being caught committing an offense. Reintegrating offenders back into a school community requires a restorative process to deal with this experience of shame (Braithwaite, 1989). It cannot perhaps be completely avoided, but a restorative process can be constructed carefully to avoid the degradation of persons that often happens in the process of excluding them. Restorative processes concentrate instead on regrading offenders as full community members on terms that also meet the needs of victims.

Increase the Number of Voices in the Conversation

Conventional justice and school discipline systems typically subject the individual offender to a process of isolation under a judicial or administrative gaze. The process moves from accusation to moral guilt. The offender is required to demonstrate remorseful and submissive behavior and to acknowledge the authorities if he is not to attract righteous anger directed at him alone. Some offenders become so skilled at making a show of remorse to authority figures that they become immune to any appreciation of the damage they have done to others. By contrast, restorative processes are not just interested in the voices of accusation and guilt. More perspectives are deliberately brought into the conversation. Rather than being isolated, the offender is wrapped in a network of those who matter to him and can support him to be accountable. Responsibility is shared among members of this network as the process works to address the harm done by the offense. At the same time, the person who has offended is still made significantly accountable. Accountability is taken very seriously, but in a more relational context than in a retributive, punishment-oriented system.

As a result of the increased number of voices, restorative conferences can be very creative at generating ideas for addressing the harm done by the offense. Ideas can emerge that would never be contemplated by school authorities. A dozen or so minds bent to the task of designing an accountability plan can come up with more creative ideas than one busy school principal. As a result, the plan to address a problem can be crafted to specifically address the needs and concerns of both the victim and the offender.

Address the Need for Relationship Healing

A restorative perspective views an offense primarily as a rupture in a relationship rather than as evidence of a moral or mental health deficit in the offender (requiring either punishment or treatment). This is a big shift from conventional thinking in justice systems. The focus shifts onto identifying the damage done to a person in a relationship, and what follows is an effort to put things right. The offense is viewed more from an *interpersonal* than from an *intrapersonal* perspective. The perpetrator of the offense may well be harmed by her own offending too. As Howard Zehr (2002) suggests, the offense is examined for the obligation it creates on the offender to repair the harm done, rather than for its indication of something wrong or deficient in the person of the offender. Restorative conferences invite offenders to attend to the consequences of their actions for others, not just for themselves, and then to act responsibly to address these consequences.

Sometimes it is difficult to realistically restore all that has been harmed by an offense. In such circumstances, it is still worthwhile to address the harm done in a symbolic way. Victims are often quite happy to understand this distinction. They frequently find solace in an apology and an assurance that something similarly harmful will not happen to anyone else in the future. Often relationship healing of this kind takes place in quite intangible ways that cannot be counted or measured.

Avoid Totalizing Language

Language uses are practices that have impact on people's lives and relationships. It makes a big difference to the outcomes of a conference if inclusive and respectful language is used. In particular, we advocate the avoidance of totalizing language because of its disrespectful nature. *Totalizing language* involves the use of words and phrases that attempt to summarize the nature of a person under a singular description. Often it emphasizes one aspect of a person's behavior and organizes others' understanding of that person around the single aspect, as if contradictory information did not exist. For example, a person hits someone and is then referred to as "violent" by nature. Further examples include the labeling of students as "behavior problems," "oppositional-defiant," "at risk," "learning disabled," or from a "dysfunctional family." The problem is that no one is violent, or a behavior problem, or dysfunctional all the time, and no single description accounts for an individual's contradictions and exceptions. Universal words such as "always" and "never" are frequently used in totalizing language. When a narrow band of experience is used to represent a person as a whole, counter stories are rendered invisible. Totalizing language used by people with authority behind them, such as teachers, counselors, or administrators, can be very powerful in its effects because it is hard for students to resist. Even when they don't like it, students often internalize these effects and come to know themselves in diminished ways, because they have been described in such ways by those with power and influence. For the person being described, as well as for others, total-izing language blinds people to the possibility of things being otherwise and therefore to the possibility of change.

Narrative practice aims to counteract the internalizing effects of totaliz-ing language through the practice of *externalizing language.* In restorative conferences, this means describing actions and behaviors as the problem, but persons (students or teachers or parents) are not called problem persons. Externalizing language is used to express profound respect for people, to avoid attributing blame, and to make room for shifts in responsibility taking.

Michael White's (1989) aphorism, repeated throughout this book, sum-marizes this perspective: "The person is not the problem; the problem is the problem" (p. 6). In restorative conferences, it can be written on a white-board and referred to as a motto to guide the conference process. The mes-sage is that offenders will be treated respectfully, and their actions will be separated from any assumption about their nature as "bad" or "sick." Instead, they will be assumed to be moral agents who can think and take responsibility for their own behavior.

On the basis of these principles, we shall now outline a process for conducting a restorative conference. We shall do this by telling a story and interrupting it along the way to point out the process being used. The story is told from the point of view of a school counselor.

A CASE VIGNETTE: A RESTORATIVE CONFERENCE

The Offending Incident

An e-mail from the deputy principal asked for help to sort out a fight among a group of girls. Apparently, one girl had called out to another girl to get her attention, and a third girl had "jumped" her from behind. The assault was very serious and many punches were thrown, hair was pulled, and there was a great deal of swearing and insults directed at the girl on the receiving end of the assault. During the investigation, the girls were required to open their school bags, and it was revealed that one girl had a piece of iron pipe in her bag. Some other students were present at the scene of the fight, and many of them recorded the fight on their mobile phones. All three girls wrote down their state-ments for the deputy principal, and they were all facing serious disciplinary charges.

The principal wanted all parties to take full responsibility for their actions and to send a strong message to the school community that this behavior was not acceptable. A fight like this would normally result in all the students involved being expelled from school, but the deputy principal felt that there were wider issues involved. To expel the students would not have any lasting benefits and may in fact cause more extensive problems because of the flow-on effects in the wider community of the potential for retribution from the respective families. She asked the counselor to set up a restorative conference to address the issues and to decide if the school board should terminate their school enrollment anyway. The students were told to stay home while the conference was set up, and their parents were informed that a conference would be called and that they would be required to attend.

How Restorative Conferences Can Be Used

Restorative conferences have been used by schools in a variety of ways. Clearly, the work to be done toward the establishing of a conference is not justified unless there is a level of seriousness that has been reached. Suspension has to be at least under consideration. Schools vary in how they use the process, however. For some, it is an alternative to the issuing of a suspension. For others, it is used after a suspension to establish the criteria for a student's return to school, or even to establish whether the student will be allowed back into the school at all. It is up to the local school or district administration to decide where best it fits in a particular context.

In order to work, a restorative conference needs the commitment of the school principal and a cooperative relationship between the principal and whoever will facilitate the conference, in this case the school counselor. Counselors would not be wise to start establishing such conferences on their own without this collaboration and commitment. Neither should a punishment process be instigated alongside a restorative conference, lest the two processes interfere with each other.

Assembling the Conference Participants

Once it was decided to proceed with the conference, I (the story is told here by the school counselor) took out my conference facilitator checklist and systematically worked through each stage. First, I compiled a list of potential participants, which included the following:

- The person who was assaulted
- The persons who assaulted her
- The supporters and family members of all of the students involved, including friends or acquaintances
- Witnesses to the event
- School officials
- The nurse who attended the girl who was assaulted
- Social workers who have contact with the girls
- The chairperson of the school board (in New Zealand, each school has its own board)
- The principal

Then I began the task of preparation for the conference. I talked to the school administrators, explained the purpose of the conference, and asked what outcomes they expected. Above all else, they wanted school to be a safe place and for these young people and their parents to assure the school that they would do all they could to provide a safe environment. Should this outcome not be achieved, then the offenders should be excluded permanently from school.

Then I interviewed the young people and explained the purpose of the conference and what would be required of them and their parents. I asked them to read out their statement (the one they had written for the deputy principal) and review what they had written. Then we discussed what they had not included in their formal statement, and I wrote these things down. I carefully explained that if they walked out of the conference or refused to attend, then the opportunity to resolve the issues would be lost and the school would have to implement formal disciplinary procedures.

I explained that I would help to manage any strong emotions that might come up during discussions. If this did happen, it was important for everyone to see how people had been affected by what happened at school.

I gave them a list of the questions that they would be asked and told them we would meet in the school library at 6:00 p.m. in three days.

I then interviewed the teachers who had broken up the fight. For this interview, I adapted a standard line of questions:

- How did you become involved?
- What happened?
- What has happened since?
- How has this situation affected you?
- What are the issues that concern you the most?
- What would you like to see happen as a result of this conference?

Next, I contacted the parents, explained the purpose and process of the conference, and spoke of the possible benefits it could bring. I also mentioned the alternatives being considered if the conference did not go well. I asked them similar questions to the ones I asked the teachers because I didn't want any surprises. I requested that they "speak from their hearts" at the conference and resist the temptation to put anyone down or label anyone. They were given an information sheet that covered the points I was making. I had to convince the parents of the girl who was assaulted to suspend their desire to file charges with the police until they could experience the conference and its outcomes. The police officer they had spoken to could, however, be invited to participate in the conference. I explained how the conference would more than likely produce better outcomes than punishment would achieve. I informed them that they should allow at least 2 hours for the conference. Finally, I asked if they would like to open with any culturally relevant ritual.

Some parents had trouble organizing babysitters, others were concerned about transportation, and others had to coordinate time off work. Some teachers couldn't come at short notice, but in the end a conference was organized.

The Importance of Preparation

This preparation work is critical for the success of a restorative conference. There can be several hours of professional and clerical work involved. Although it seems as if this work is considerable, there are many ways to streamline the process. Clerical staff, for example, can deal with the routine tasks of contacting family members and using checklists, or conduct the preliminary interviews. In some schools, a staff member has time allocated and responsibility for setting up conferences. Once a system is established, the pre-conference process can be done smoothly and efficiently. Schools have to decide who will be the best person to do it. Some of the work requires professional skill beyond clerical work.

For the most successful conferences, there has to be buy-in from the local community. This means thinking carefully about relationship building so that the invitation to attend does not come across as an authoritarian demand but still conveys the seriousness of the situation. Some schools have hesitated for some time before being willing to undertake such work. But when they had done a few conferences, the enthusiasm for tackling problems in this way started to grow, and they began holding more conferences at more frequent intervals.

Preparing for the Conference

I thought long and hard about this conference. I knew there was a history of trouble between the families, and that had been the reason for including the police officer. I knew also that there was reluctance from some teachers about attending the conference. The teacher who had interrupted the fight was skeptical about the efficacy of conferences and felt that the school should have expelled the offending students right there and then.

I arranged for coffee, tea, and biscuits to be available at the end of the meeting. This would be the time when participants would be chatting over a hot drink, while I would be free to finalize the agreement and produce copies of it for all those present.

On the day of the conference, I drew up a seating plan. The instigators of the assault and their parents and supporters would sit on one side of the circle, and the other families would sit facing them on the other side. The deputy principal would sit at the top of the circle, and the teachers and social worker around the sides between the families.

I thought carefully about the order of speaking and what I would do if there was any intimidation of participants. Before people arrived, I reviewed the process I would use to ensure respectful ways of speaking. On the whiteboard, I wrote in large letters, "The person is not the problem; the problem is the problem."

As the meeting approached, I went over my checklist (see Box 6.1) one last time. I decided to group the families of the offenders and the girl who had been assaulted on separate sides of the library while all the participants arrived. I asked the deputy principal to welcome one group and the principal to welcome the other. When everyone was assembled, I directed them to their allocated seats.

BOX 6.1
THE CONFERENCE PROCESS

1. Write on the whiteboard, "The person is not the problem; the problem is the problem."

2. Begin with a cultural ritual, as appropriate.

3. Establish ground rules.

4. Ask each person to introduce himself or herself and say one thing he or she hopes will come from the conference.

5. Ask senior school official to state what the offense was and why the conference was called. Ask offender to agree that this is what happened.

6. Name the problem. Each participant says what the problem is from his or her perspective.

7. Write these names for the problem in a circle on the whiteboard.

8. Do another round in which each person is asked, "What has been the effect of the problem on you?"

9. Draw another circle on the whiteboard.

10. Ask for times, places, and relationships where the problem is not present.

11. Ask what new descriptions of the people become possible when we look at these exceptions to the problem story.

12. Ask the offender which of the two stories, represented by the two circles drawn on the whiteboard, he or she would like to be known by in the future.

13. Ask the victim(s) what needs to be set right in order for the harm done by the problem to be addressed.

14. Ask everyone to contribute to a list of ideas for setting things right.

15. Check that the plan drawn up addresses the concerns of the victim(s).

16. Assign responsibility for each element of the plan.

17. End with thanks and with a small celebration.

Source: Adapted from Restorative practices development team (2004). *Restorative practices in schools.* University of Waikato.

The Conference Itself

I welcomed the group and thanked them for their participation. I explained the purpose of the meeting. I then invited a representative of the families to say an opening *karakia* (a Maori cultural invocation, which is like a prayer).

I reminded everyone that the meeting would focus on the incident at school and that we would seek to understand how people had been affected. We would then discuss what needed to be done to make amends and put things right. I reminded them that the meeting was not a trial and asked for agreement on some important ground rules (listening, no intimidation of others, not interrupting, no name-calling, respecting privacy).

The deputy principal spoke first about the offense that had led to the conference and why the school was treating this matter very seriously. I then turned to the girl who had done the assault and asked her to first agree that what the deputy principal had said was accurate and then to tell the meeting what had happened. With a bit of prompting, she explained what had led up to the assault and how she had become involved. I asked her to explain what she had been thinking at the time she assaulted the girl. The same questions were asked of the other girl who had played a role in the assault.

Then I turned to the girl who had been assaulted and asked for her story of what had happened. When she had finished, I asked her to sum up in a few words what the problem was all about. I went around the room and asked each person present to do the same—name the problem in a few words. Each name was written on the whiteboard in the middle of the circle. I took care not to write down a person as a problem but to use externalizing language and name the problem itself. Names that emerged referred to different perspectives on the problem incident: *a planned attack, cell phone recording, fighting, an ongoing battle, unacceptable violence on the school grounds, vicious behavior, gossiping and back-stabbing, criminal assault, calculated violence,* and so on. Each description was accepted and written down in the circle. The main perpetrator of the assault was also asked to name the problem. She looked ashamed and said nothing. I thanked everyone for their suggestions and said, "Actually, all that is written in the circle is the problem, since it contains how the problem looks from everyone's perspective."

Mapping the Effects of the Problem

Next, I instigated another round to inquire into the effects of the problem on each person present. I began with the girl who was the victim of the assault. She spoke of her injuries and her embarrassment, and her mother added that she had missed 2 days of school and had been afraid to return in case something happened again. I asked her parents to both speak about the effect of the problem on them. They were both angry and also worried about what was happening among girls who used to get along much better. The father was also outraged that this could have happened on the school grounds.

As each person talked, I drew spokes out from the circle that contained the names for the problem and recorded in a few words what the effects of the problem were. For example, I wrote *two days off school, fear, worry, anger, bruising and grazes,* and so on.

The next step was to address the supporters of the girls who led the assault. I acknowledged how difficult it must be for them to hear these stories and asked them the same question about the effects of the problem on them personally. One parent was angry at her daughter and had punished her at home when she found out the story. Another expressed anger at the victim as well for the ongoing battle that had led to this latest incident.

Others in the circle were asked the same question, and the teachers, social worker, and principal each spoke briefly of how the assault had affected them personally. Some were saddened, some shocked, and some worried about the effects on other students. One had gone home and wondered about whether she was in the right job because she found this incident so disturbing to witness. The principal spoke sincerely about how important it was to her for the school to be safe for all students, and how it saddened her that the reputation of the school had been severely damaged as word of the assault had filtered into the community. She explained how a good school reputation meant that she would be able to attract better staff, and that meant better teaching and learning for students.

As each person contributed, his or her words were written on the whiteboard on the end of the spokes emanating from the circle that contained the problem. I ended by asking the girls who had participated in the assault how the problem had affected them. They needed a little help to articulate it, but one spoke about feeling bad, the other about being confused; both were in trouble at home, and both were afraid of being thrown out of the school.

I then asked the whole group, "What is it like to see all of these effects of this problem written up here?"

There were various comments in response, mostly about how it was a shock to see that so many people had been affected.

Opening the Counter Story

At this point, I said, "So what we have here on the whiteboard represents the problem story we are here to set right. But no problem story ever tells us all that we need to know about anyone. What can anyone here tell us about these two girls [who perpetrated the assault] that does not fit with this problem story?"

There was a brief silence, and then one of the teachers spoke about how one of the girls had shown kindness and willingness to stick up for another student who had been bullied. I drew another circle on the whiteboard, and this time worked from the outside of the circle. I drew a spoke out from it and wrote on the end of it *Helped a student who was being bullied*.

"What does this example say about her?" I asked.

"Well, it shows that she can be protective of others," said the father of one of the victims. I wrote *Protective of others* in the middle of the circle.

Slowly, other examples emerged of the two girls as showing responsible behavior at home, being good students, being loyal team members, and so on. The girl who had been assaulted added that all three girls had been in the same class 2 years earlier and had gotten along fine at that time.

When the second circle diagram was completed, I stood back and spoke directly to the two girls who had perpetrated the assault.

"Here is a problem story," I said, "and here is another story. In future, which one would you like to be the story that everyone knows about you?"

Without hesitation, both girls pointed with relief to the positive story.

"So in order to show that you are serious," I added, "I would like to invite you to put right some of the damage that was done by the problem story."

Addressing the Harm

It was now time to address in earnest the question of repairing the harm that had been done.

I asked both of the girls who had done the assault whether, after they had heard how everybody had been affected, they had anything they wanted to say to the other girl or her family or to anyone else. Each in turn apologized for what she had done both to the girl and her family and to the school authorities.

Then I turned to the family of the girl who had been assaulted and asked if they were satisfied that the harm that had been done had been fully acknowledged.

The father of the girl responded, "Yes, I hear that they have owned up to what they did and, here at this meeting, that is fine. But how can we be sure what will happen tomorrow and next week? Words are fine, but we need to know that their actions will be different."

I thanked him for raising this question and agreed that an apology was only as good as the actions that proved it sincere. I then asked the two girls who had perpetrated the assault and the rest of the group what else was needed to repair the harm and ensure that it would not happen again. I said I would list on the whiteboard a series of actions that we could all take to make certain this did not happen again.

The mother of one of the girls suggested she could pick both girls up from school at the end of each day and be there when the girls were coming out of school so that no opportunity for fighting would develop.

Concern was expressed about other students expecting the conflict to continue, and the meeting decided that one of the teachers would host a ritual meeting the following week in which a formal apology would be made to the victim of the assault, witnessed by four friends chosen by each of the three girls. The girls also agreed that anyone who asked what happened at the restorative conference would be told that it was over and that the families had sorted it all out.

One of the mothers suggested that the girls write an apology letter to those affected by the assault and that the school could keep a copy of it on file for future reference. The girls agreed to this, and the counselor offered to assist them to write this letter.

The cell phone recordings of the fight by an unknown number of students were raised by the mother of the victim. She was concerned that the recording could be used to publicize the assault and to continue the conflict. The meeting agreed that there was little anyone could do to prevent its distribution on the Internet and to other students' phones.

The principal suggested making a statement to the whole school about the assault, and she would also mention the inappropriate use of cell phones. She told the parents that cell phones were not allowed to be used in class or they would be confiscated until the end of the day. She also agreed to address this matter in a school newsletter to parents. She would also use a school assembly to make clear that bringing any form of weapon to school was unacceptable and that, if any student felt unsafe at school, he or she should talk to someone who could help, rather than take the law into the person's own hands.

As counselor, I suggested that I would be willing to meet with all three girls once a week for 4 weeks on Friday at lunchtime to talk through differences among them.

The deputy principal said that he would be asking the girls' teachers to give a weekly report on their behavior in class.

The mother of the victim agreed to check with her daughter every day for the next month about any reoccurring problems and to phone the school immediately about any issues.

I asked the principal if she was satisfied that the conference had addressed her initial concern about whether to terminate the enrollment of the students involved in the assault. She thought for a long time before turning and asking the parents of the girl who had been assaulted whether they were satisfied with the outcomes of the conference.

The parents felt that no good would be achieved by expelling the students, as their future would be damaged by such an action. They asked their daughter if she could honestly feel safe at school and could get back to her studies. The daughter believed that she could, if everyone did what they had said they would do. The principal then stated that, if the parents were satisfied and their daughter was satisfied, she would consider the matter of expulsion closed, as long as the action plan was followed.

A list of all the actions to be taken was written up as the plan to put things right. As the conference was drawing to a close, I summarized what had been agreed on and checked that there was nothing left to say.

The final thing was to decide who would monitor the agreement before formally closing the meeting. It was decided that the deputy principal would do this in consultation with the parents. This decision was added to the plan (see Box 6.2).

BOX 6.2
OUTCOME OF MEETING

- The girls will tell all those who ask about the fight that it is over and that the families have sorted it out.
- The mother of one of the girls agrees that she will pick both girls (those who perpetrated the assault) up from school at the end of each day.
- A teacher will hold a meeting where apologies are given and received.

- The girls will write an apology letter with assistance from the guidance counselor and give it to all those affected by their actions. A copy will be kept in their individual files.
- The principal will address the whole school through an assembly on appropriate use of cell phones.
- The principal will also address this issue in a newsletter to parents.
- The counselor will meet the three girls once a week for 4 weeks on Friday at lunchtime for mediation.
- The deputy principal will monitor the girls' behavior on a weekly basis through reports from class teachers.
- The mother of the victim will check with her daughter every day for the next month about reoccurring problems and phone the school immediately about any issues.
- The deputy principal will monitor the plan and contact parents after 2 weeks to advise of progress and again after a further 2 weeks.

"What happens if the agreement doesn't hold?" one of the parents asked.

I turned to the principal and she said decisively, "If it doesn't hold, then the girls will be suspended pending a Board of Trustees meeting."

"Does everyone understand that?" I asked.

The whole meeting nodded in agreement. I thanked them warmly for their contributions and told them I appreciated the way they had all participated.

I then invited all those present to say anything they liked about the restorative conference.

The parents spoke first: "Our daughter had brought shame on our family, and we didn't bring up our kids in this way. We are sorry to the mother of the girl our daughters gave a hiding to. We want to say sorry to the principal for this trouble. We want our kids to learn how to study. They already know how to fight!"

"We shall keep a closer eye on our girls now. We don't want any trouble, but it's been good that we could talk. Thanks for going to the trouble of setting it up. I didn't really want to come, but I am glad I did. Now it's up to us to see that our kids come to school to learn. We will make sure they stick to the agreement because we think this is a good school."

"There is enough violence in our community without it coming into school. It's been good to realize that the school cares about our kids. I didn't know my daughter was a leader. It's a good thing."

Then the social worker thanked us for setting up the conference, and a teacher expressed hope that the school could rely on the parents to impress on their daughters that there is no place for violence at school.

One of the girls said, "I was scared to come but I had to. I don't like getting into this trouble. I was good at first, but I have let my parents down. I am sorry."

Another girl said, "I wish I had not listened to the others and made up my own mind. I didn't realize it was this serious. I thought it was only a hiding, [but] now I can see how many people have been affected. I just want to get on with school now."

Finally, the family representative who had opened with a *karakia* closed the meeting in the same way.

SUMMARY

In this chapter, we have introduced the process of a restorative conference and illustrated it with a case vignette. What seems like a long process is justified in terms of its powerful effects. Such a conference has longer-lasting effects than expelling the students and shifting the problem to somewhere else. In this case, it would have been unlikely that the families would ever have spoken to each other again, except to continue hostilities. The education of their daughters would have suffered significantly. Various supporters of each side in the dispute would have continued to reignite the conflict as a face-saving measure, and the education of all the girls would have suffered. By contrast, in this real-life case, all the students are still in school years after the event. While they are not close friends, they are all actively involved in their class work.

The restorative conference draws upon the logic of restorative justice work in the criminal justice system. It is based on the relational perspective that an offense is primarily an offense against another person rather than against the authority of the rules. Recognizing this principle leads to a practice of addressing the harm done and putting it right, rather than resorting to punishments that often do not lead to change.

QUESTIONS FOR REFLECTION

1. Have you ever had an offense committed against you? What would have restored or repaired the harm that was done to you?

2. Think of an offense you have witnessed in a school that was handled through retributive justice. What could have happened if a restorative conference had been used?

3. Imagine a conflict in your school. Who has been impacted by the conflict that might have a vested interest in seeing the harm addressed?

4. With the same conflict, prepare a possible restorative conference. Using the restorative conference checklist, what steps would you take to prepare for a successful meeting?

5. How can the principles of a restorative conference be adapted to fit differences in age, culture, and school setting?

QUESTIONS FOR RESEARCH

1. What are the comparative financial and emotional costs for school communities of addressing offenses through retributive measures or through restorative conferences?

2. What are the comparative rates of reoffending after a restorative conference and a standard punishment?

3. What are the impacts of a restorative conference on
   (a) students' academic progress?
   (b) classroom relationships?
   (c) ongoing behavior by the person who did the offending?
   (d) school climate?

4. Investigate a single case study of a restorative conference in depth. What happens? What meaning does it have for all concerned?

5. Does the incorporation of restorative conferences into a school impact on the way in which teachers, counselors, and administrators speak, think, or write about students?

7

Restorative Practices

PRINCIPLES OF PUTTING IT RIGHT

In the last chapter, we outlined a conferencing process that can be used for serious disciplinary offenses. However, not all offending behavior is serious enough to justify the commitment and expense of such a conference. There seems, moreover, little point in waiting until things get to the most serious level before starting to implement the principles of restorative practice. These principles can be applied to good effect at much more basic levels than at the most serious and dramatic. They can be applied as less formal, less time-consuming, low-level interventions, rather than waiting to use them as a last resort. Potentially, they can even prevent matters escalating to a point where a suspension is even being considered.

Which principles are we talking about? The most basic principle of restorative practices is to think in terms of relationships, rather than in terms of individuals. Especially when someone does something wrong, it is possible to think more in terms of harm done in a relationship than in terms of rules being broken or authority being damaged. It follows that the response to offending from teachers, administrators, and counselors will change. Instead of resorting to retributive punishments, the response needs to focus first on an effort to invite those involved to address the harm done to a relationship by a problematic behavior. To state it simply, the underlying injunction implied by all restorative practices is to *"put it right!"*

By contrast, punishment does not help the victim of a person's offending behavior. It hurts the offender and aims to teach a moral lesson. But often this lesson appears to be (at best) internalized in the offender, rather than applied to relationships with others. The implicit message is often, "Do better next time." No responsibility for putting right the damage done *this time* is necessarily required. Usually, no one other than the offender stands to benefit from the punishment. There may be a hope that things will be put right, but there is little concerted effort to ensure this happens.

What does it take to focus on addressing relationship harm and putting it right? The first requirement is not to isolate the offender (a common approach in retributive justice) but to keep him in conversation with those affected by the offense. The role of the professional worker, perhaps the school counselor, but it could be a teacher as well (see below), is not to take on the task of defending the rules but to facilitate a reconstructive conversation between the offender and those who have been affected by the offense. If there is a direct victim, this person needs to be identified and given a voice in speaking about how actions of the offender hurt him. If there are others who have been affected by the offending behavior more indirectly, they too can be invited into the community of care around the problem and given a chance to have a voice.

The initial focus of conversation needs to be on the relational effects of the problem. Note that the concentration on the effects is different from identifying the underlying causes of the offense. Causes lie in the past and are often too complex to tease out. Even when they are identified, often nothing much changes. Identifying causes looks backward. Investigating effects points forward to the future, which is where things can be put right.

The narrative practice of externalizing helps name the offense and avoid the deficit logic of making the person into the problem. Tracing the effects of the offense involves asking questions that map the effects of the problem so that the harm done by the offending behavior is clarified. Those affected can then be asked what would minimize or remove the harm done to them. The offender can then be invited to take up responsibility and to put things right. In narrative terms, this last step opens up an alternative story to the story of the offense.

The best way to understand how this process can work is to illustrate it with a story that occurred in a high school. It is an example of a relatively brief restorative conversation that happens very quickly after a relatively minor offense that nevertheless caused disruption in a class. Here the person who facilitates the restorative conversation is a teacher trained in restorative practices.

A CASE VIGNETTE: THE PUSH

The teacher was on the other side of the room helping a student with her work. Out of the corner of her eye, she saw Paki get up out of his chair and go over to George and push him sharply.

"Excuse me," she said to the girl she was helping. She walked swiftly over to the boys and said assertively, "Go back to your chair and sit down now. You know this is unacceptable, and I want you both to wait after the bell rings to talk about this disturbance to our lesson."

"I saw it, Miss," another boy offered.

"This matter is not open for discussion," she said firmly.

The class settled back to work, although there was palpable tension in the room. The teacher continued to teach the class without referring to the recent disturbance.

At the end of the lesson, the two boys shuffled up to her as the rest of the class was leaving.

She looked both boys in the eyes and said, "This may take a few minutes or it may take longer, in which case you must come back here at lunchtime. I am going to ask you both some questions about what I saw to see if we can sort it out now."

She turned to Paki and said, "What happened?"

"I had heard that he was going to give me a hiding after school and so I pushed him."

She turned her attention to the other boy. "George, what were you thinking when it happened?"

"I was shocked and surprised. I wasn't expecting it. I was just sitting doing my work, and he came over to me and pushed me off my chair. It was only a rumor that I was going to give him a hiding after school."

She looked back at Paki. "What were you thinking when you pushed him?" she asked.

"I wanted to show him I was not scared," he replied.

"What has the whole incident had you thinking about since it happened?"

"I shouldn't have pushed him during class, but I wanted everyone to see I wasn't scared of him."

"What has the incident got you thinking about since being pushed?" she asked George.

"I didn't know what it was about and I wanted to get up and punch him back. I had done nothing."

"How has the incident affected you?" she asked.

"I feel angry and mad because of it. I feel shamed as well."

"What's been the worst part of it for you?" she inquired.

"I never wanted trouble but now I don't care. The other kids were laughing. It's the shame of it."

She turned to Paki and said, "Who else do you think has been affected by the incident?"

The boy thought a while and said, "Well, everyone in the class, at least the ones who saw it."

"Anyone else?" she probed.

"You as well. It stopped you teaching for a while, and I don't think the class was the same afterward."

"How were all those whom you mentioned affected by the incident?"

This question took a bit longer to answer.

"I dunno," he shrugged, "I suppose they were wondering what was gonna happen next. I suppose they couldn't concentrate."

"This incident has clearly affected many people in this class, including me. You are right. It prevented me from teaching for a while during the lesson."

The teacher asked Paki, "What do you need to do to make things right?"

He looked down at the floor and mumbled, "I need to apologize to George for hitting him and to you for causing a drama."

"Would you like to do that now?" she asked.

Paki stood up slightly and reached out his hand to shake George's hand.

"Sorry," he said. He looked up at his teacher. "Sorry," he said again.

She knew that it was a big step for him to apologize in this way, so she accepted his apology.

"Thank you, Paki," she said.

She looked at George and asked him the same question. "What do you need to do or to ask for to make things right?"

"I need to know that this is not going to keep on going. I just want things to get back to normal," George said.

"Okay. How can we make sure that this kind of thing doesn't happen again?" she asked.

"It won't happen again, Miss, you can be sure of that," Paki ventured. "If I hear that George wants a fight, I will ask him directly and not listen to what others are saying."

"And George, how can we make sure this doesn't happen again?"

"I will tell my friends that it's sorted now," George said.

"I would like you both to come to the front of the class and apologize to them next time we meet, because this disturbance affected everyone. Thank you both for discussing this matter and for resolving the conflict."

With the support of the teacher, the two boys apologized to the class. They ended up becoming good friends afterward, and the class worked well together for the rest of the year. The teacher saw this as an opportunity for everyone to learn some important principles about how relationships can be exposed to rumor and trouble and, throughout the year, she drew upon this experience a number of times to remind the class how they could learn positive lessons from everyday events.

Highlights of the Story

Several things should be highlighted in this story. First of all, rather than telling the boys what was wrong, the teacher asked questions to uncover the harm that had been caused. The students were treated with dignity and respect, rather than shamed. They were asked questions that assumed they are capable moral agents with worthwhile things to say.

Second, the idea of the apology does not originate from the teacher. It is offered by the boys, in response to her questions. It is also graciously accepted in a way that cements it in as a relational event. It can be said now to be a plot development in the relationship story of the class.

Third, attention is paid to the effects of the problem incident on others who witnessed it, and their concerns are included, rather than ignored, in the effort to put things right. In this instance, they are not given an actual voice in the conversation, but what they might say is easily imagined by the other protagonists. On other occasions, the voice of a significant witness might be included in the conversation. Other class members are included in the whole-class apology, however. The effect of the incident on them is acknowledged.

Fourth, by the end of a brief conversation, a potentially explosive issue has been effectively dealt with. Ignored, it would likely have festered and grown. It was not difficult for the teacher to do, as she was more or less rehearsing a script provided during a training event. Some teachers even have this script on a laminated paper and follow the prompts with equally successful results. Then, after a few of these restorative conversations, they put the script away and focus on the shifts in the relationships that occur. Once they develop confidence in the process, they start to just focus on the outcome of putting things right. What is needed by teachers is a desire to think more carefully about the centrality of relationships in their teaching.

Finally, the task of putting things right is far more demanding, emotionally and morally, than most punishments would have been. It is not coerced, so much as produced by a dialogue, and then taken up within that dialogue. At the same time, the relationship between the teacher and the students involved is not only preserved but also strengthened by the resolution. Indeed, the resolution seems to have ongoing positive effects.

The whole thing can be said to be an educational experience for the boys and for others in the class, especially when we take a broad view of education as preparing children and young people to become responsible citizens. The restorative process is saturated with respect. It is both modeled and experienced by the participants in the conversation, even in a circumstance where peaceful relations have been under threat.

For the teacher also, learning is likely to take place. Through effective listening, she learns about the boys she is teaching, and about what concerns and motivates them, in ways she might not have known before. She does this by showing respect for what they have to say. Since good teaching is dependent on the efficacy of the teacher–student relationship, potentially she is able to be a more effective teacher with these boys (and with the class) as a result.

This approach is sustainable and does not require lots of money or lots of training. It can be introduced easily at the beginning of the school year to all interested staff by a person trained in restorative practices. Then it's just a matter of teachers using it and experimenting with the questions and not being afraid to try this approach. Moreover, this approach maintains the integrity of the teacher and of her relationships with students throughout, in a way that punishment never could.

THE RESTORATIVE PROCESS

There is always a risk in laying out a process in a linear fashion. To do so simplifies the process and makes it look neat and tidy. Yet conversations are messy affairs, which seldom proceed according to the map. The risk is that people will either stick rigidly to the map and find that it does not fit what is happening in a real-life conversation, or they will diverge off the path that is on the map and get lost. In either case, there is a danger that the map will quickly be declared useless and the process will be abandoned as a waste of time.

On the other hand, in order to learn to use a new process, we usually need some kind of map if we are not to get lost before we have started. Moreover, it is in the nature of maps for them to be simplifications. Useful maps will strike a balance between being too simplistic on the one hand and too complex on the other. One of the most important uses of a map is to serve as a guide when we are uncertain about which direction to take. Having some kind of map in mind is necessary for a conversation to be purposeful. It quells anxiety and offers a point of reference in the moments when one realizes a conversation has gotten off track and is wandering around in the bushes.

We therefore offer a map for a restorative conversation, along with an invitation to use it intelligently rather than copy it slavishly. This means using it as a checklist to refer to at the start of a conversation and along the way as a reference to answer the internal question, "Where are we up to?" Since conversations are complex rather than linear, it should be acknowledged that sometimes it may be necessary to cycle through what the map refers to twice, or even three or four times.

Stage 1: Establishing the Conversation

The tasks at this stage are to decide who will be part of the conversation and to establish a time and place for it to occur. In the example above, the teacher included the person who did the push and the person on the receiving end—the victim. At the simplest end of the continuum, these two may be enough to deal with a small incident. The important thing is that a relationship where some harm has occurred is the focus. Often, however, there is profit in widening the circle a bit further and including another student, perhaps a bystander. Or another teacher may be included. Or a parent of the offender and of the victim may be willing to be part of the conversation. The question is, "Who is affected by what happened?" And therefore, "Who has a stake in seeing things put right?"

The conversation needs to take place at a time and place where people can talk without interruption. This should not be in front of a class and should not be pressured by immediate time demands. We are not suggesting that hours of time need to be set aside. A conversation such as the one above can take place within a few minutes.

Stage 2: Identifying the Problem

Once the participants in the conversation have been brought together, the task of addressing what has happened begins. The story of what took place needs to be told and the different perspectives on it heard and acknowledged. In the example above, the teacher is careful not to locate either of the parties as the cause of the problem. The problem is named as a relational event and referred to, using externalizing language, as "the incident." It is not called, for example, something like "Paki losing his temper," because that would internalize the problem in one of the boys and would make it harder for it to be seen as a relational event.

Stage 3: Mapping the Effects of the Problem

The next stage involves tracing the effects of the problem on all stakeholders. Sometimes this is made easier by actually drawing a diagram like a map. The circle diagram with the spokes emerging from it, as described in the previous chapter, can be used in smaller conversations like this as well. The names for the problem are placed in the center of the circle, and each of the spokes emerging from the circle is used to refer to the effects of the problem on one person. These effects may be emotional ("How did it get you to feel?"), cognitive ("What did it get you thinking?"), behavioral ("What did it get you to do?"), and relational ("How did it affect things between you?"). Notice that "it" is the origin of each effect in the languaging of the relationship between the problem and the persons.

Importantly, the effects are traced beyond the immediate consciousness of the central protagonists. In the story above, the teacher and others in the class are also affected by the incident, and the effects on each of them are made subject to inquiry. These others can often speak for themselves about these effects, and certainly every person present for the conversation should be asked about the effects on them. However, the effects of what happened on others can also be imagined by those present.

The important thing is for the conversation to increase everyone's understanding of how the effects of a conflict ripple outward. They are seldom contained within the experience of the immediate protagonists. A key difference here between restorative practices and retributive thinking is that the school authorities should not monopolize the definition of these effects. In other words, teachers and administrators should avoid insisting that every little offense is an offense against the school rules. Each offense should instead be understood primarily as a relational rather than an institutional event, and care should be taken to facilitate an inquiry into its relational effects.

Stage 4: Addressing the Harm

Once a full account of the harm has been given, an obligation is created to do something about it. The conversation can turn to what can be done to put things right. If one person has harmed another, this person can be asked to pick up the mantle of responsibility and put things right.

It helps to ask all those involved, including the person who has committed the offense, "What do you think of this problem having all of these effects? Is that okay with you?" If the answer is no, then you can ask, "Why is that? What is wrong with the incident having all these effects?" If the answer is yes, you can raise the stakes by asking, "So would you mind if things were to keep on like this or get worse, or if other people did this to you as well?"

We are then at the point where a preferred story can be opened up. It is useful to inquire about this first in general terms by asking, "In order to put things right, what would need to happen?" The offender and the victim are asked the same question. It can be followed up differently, however, with each of them. The victim can be asked, "What would you need to happen for this incident to be over and its effects on you to be addressed?" And the offender can be asked, "What are you willing to do to put things right?" Others present can also participate in this conversation. They can be asked for their ideas about putting things right, and they can also be asked, "What contribution can you make to things being put right?"

Stage 5: Forming the Plan

Out of the responses to the conversation in Stage 4 above, a list of actions that are agreed to can be drawn up. It needs to be specific about who will do what, when, and where. And it needs to include a plan for reviewing whether the plan was followed up, because putting things right must be more than pretty words. An apology is only as good as the actions in which it is embodied. In narrative terms, one way to state this is to say that an apology is not the end of a story but the beginning of one—that is, the beginning of a story of better relationship. Participants should always be asked to follow an apology with what they will do to carry it forward.

GUIDELINES FOR A RESTORATIVE CONVERSATION

	Stage	Examples of questions to ask
1	Establishing the conversation	Who is affected by what happened? Who has a stake in seeing things put right?
2	Identifying the problem	What happened? What part did you play? What can we call it? What drew you into this trouble?
3	Mapping the effects	How did it get you to feel? What did it get you to do? What did it get you thinking? How did it affect the way you are with each other? How have other people been affected?
4	Addressing the harm	What do you think of the way that this incident has affected people? Are you happy with that? Was it fair? *To the victim:* If this situation were to be put right, what would you need? *To the aggressor:* How could we make sure this doesn't happen again?
5	Forming the plan	Who will do what? When and where? How will we know it is done?

Responding to Minor Squabbles

The story of a restorative conversation we have outlined above is not as serious and extensive as the story of the offense dealt with in the restorative conference in the previous chapter. But there are many little squabbles that take place in a school community that are at a lower level still. Sometimes these result in minor physical contact but often in insults and angry exchanges. These too can be responded to with restorative practices. Teachers trained in restorative practices can intervene and conduct a quick conversation that addresses the harm done and helps students put it right.

The secret, as we have outlined above, is to focus on the relationship damage, rather than on a punitive response. The teacher does not so much need to demonstrate the authority to overpower as the authority to facilitate change. A few simple questions that treat the problem as the problem and not the persons can make a big difference quickly. Here are some examples of questions that might be asked:

- What is this squabble getting you both to do?
- How did it get control of you?
- What effect is it having?
- Is this squabble getting you to do things against your better judgment?
- What would you rather was happening?
- What would put things right?
- Are you willing to do that?
- Is that the end of the matter, or do you need to do anything else?
- Do I need to talk with you further at lunchtime?

Each of these questions can be answered very quickly, and the whole thing can be done in 3 to 5 minutes. If successful, an ongoing sore is prevented from opening up. If individuals are unwilling to address relational harm in this way, then a referral for a further step in the situation may be called for.

It remains in this chapter to expand on the spirit of restorative practices. For a fuller discussion of this brief account we refer readers to work by Wendy Drewery (2004) and by Kathy Cronin-Lampe and Ron Cronin-Lampe (2010). It is all very well to outline some practices for addressing offending behavior, but these practices cannot be effective unless there is a willingness to see them as part of an ethos in a school community. In the end, restorative practices contain within them an incipient vision of what a school community might be. They are more than simply a tool for ensuring discipline is maintained or behavior is managed (positively or otherwise). They are an expression of a community that sets out to care for its youngest members and to engage them in caring for each other. Schools that embrace this mission are not just putting things right in order to produce better test scores. They are seeking to prepare better citizens.

The focus on responsibility for how others are affected by our actions is both implicitly learned through this kind of process as well as consciously embraced. Restorative relationships are in the long run relationships of respect. By respect, we mean the willingness to always treat the other as a moral agent, capable of meaningful action, rather than as deserving to have this right taken away by punishments that do little more than demonstrate the power of the mighty. In a diverse society, some of the greatest challenges to this vision of a school community come across lines of difference. It is hardest to show respect to people with whom we differ, sometimes in fundamental ways. Learning to do this in situations of conflict is, we suspect, the best place to learn to practice respect. There is potential not just for individuals to benefit from such learning, but also for benefits to accrue to a community as a whole.

SUMMARY

In this chapter, we began by outlining some principles of restorative practice: (a) thinking in terms of harm done to relationships rather than to individuals or to authority, (b) including more voices rather than isolating the offender, (c) concentrating on the effects of an action rather than the causes, and (d) addressing the harm rather than punishing.

The chapter continued with a case vignette in which a teacher put these principles in practice. Then it went on to outline a five-stage process for a restorative conversation that featured establishing the conversation, identifying the problem, mapping the effects, addressing the harm, and forming the plan.

The chapter ended with some comments on the ethos of care that this process engenders and on which it relies.

QUESTIONS FOR REFLECTION

1. Think of examples of problematic incidents in your school. What are the implications for each one of thinking about harm done to relationships rather than about restoring authority?

2. How would you train teachers to use the Guidelines for a Restorative Conversation?

3. How would you deal with skepticism from teachers about using these questions?

4. How could you work with this process where there is a "minor" squabble between young children? What adaptations would you make to the "script"?

5. Who would assume the responsibility for training staff and the monitoring of the effects of the changes?

QUESTIONS FOR RESEARCH

1. How could you show that using these approaches had led to a difference in the relationships in your school?

2. How much time is required to address relationship problems through restorative practices? How much time is saved by addressing relationship problems through restorative practices so that they do not lead to repeat referrals? How could this be measured?

3. How could you document use of these practices in order to develop and refine the process?

8

Circle Conversations

Relationships among students in a class are the context for all school learning. When they are riven by conflict, it is not just the personal relationships that become casualties. Learning suffers as well. In this chapter, we shall discuss an approach to conflict resolution that does not focus on one particular relationship but instead addresses the whole nexus of relationships within a classroom. It uses a conversational format that rearranges the lines of force that feed a conflict within groups of students in a class and opens up the opportunity for peace-building work to occur. It is called circle time.

Circle time can be used for a variety of conversational purposes, but here we introduce it for the purpose of restoring relationships harmed by niggling conflicts among many students in a class. Sometimes many students in a class are participating in the relationship problems. Establishing a structured conversation around a circle about such problems allows every student's voice to be heard. It is an efficient use of professional time because it has the potential to interrupt relationship patterns that, left alone, can expand into bullying, behavior problems, and significant learning interference. A problem in a class may first come to the notice of a school administrator who recognizes the value of a circle conversation and invites the counselor to implement the approach.

THE HISTORY AND PURPOSES OF CIRCLE CONVERSATIONS

Many indigenous cultures throughout time have used circles to solve problems, to discuss matters affecting the tribe or community, or to resolve conflict. In New Zealand, Maori *hui* (meetings) often follow a circle format. In Canada, indigenous models of circle conversations have been developed into restorative justice practices (Stuart, 1997). In many homes, the evening dinner table is the place where family members unload the events of the day and discuss around the table the little things that have happened.

In Britain, "quality circle time" is advocated for teaching a range of social skills, including dialogical and listening skills, and for fostering desirable behaviors in schools. Jenny Mosley and Marilyn Tew (1999) have outlined a range of uses to which circle time can be put. They also detail methods of creating a conversation in a circle. Our interest here is in one particular use of such circles: for conflict resolution.

In the United States, circle conversations are also referred to as "community circles" and are common practice in elementary schools, as in many other parts of the world. Jeanne Gibbs (Gibbs & Ushijima, 2008) uses this approach in her program called "Tribes." In her work, the emphasis is on creating a social climate in a classroom based on the principles of respect, cooperative learning, and positive interactions. However, using circles to solve problems or build meaningful relationships tends to die out at the high school level. Perhaps it is due to the structure of the classrooms, or perhaps there is an assumption that teenagers might view circle conversations as somehow only suitable for younger children. In large secondary schools, where there is much more fragmentation of the timetable and students are not learning together all day, the sense of isolation and disconnection that teenagers feel can go unnoticed by the school authorities. There is all the more reason for circles to play an important part in creating a positive school climate and contributing to a program of conflict resolution.

Circles represent an unbroken chain in which there is no beginning and no end, where each individual's contributions are equally valued, and in which the conversation can go around the circle or across it at will. Circles are inclusive. They make visible the significance of every voice. They might also be said to remove the possibility of hiding. Everyone is visible to and accountable to everyone else.

In the classroom, the structure of a circle decenters the role of the teacher, temporarily at least, and provides a shift in the relational dynamics. Teachers are freed from the role of managing the class and can become listeners to what students have to say. Circles also decenter any individual student from the position of being the dominant voice or from being shamed or blamed. The circle instead places relationships between students and between students and the teacher at the center. It recognizes that any problem in the group exists as a function of the relationships among the whole group. Just as all those in the room may have variously contributed to the development of disharmony, so too can they all contribute to solving problems that affect them all. The very structure of the circle opens up new ways of speaking and opportunities for listening to what others say. The hope is that, through this method, a new story of relationship can take hold.

Not all classroom conversations are, or even should be, structured in the format of a circle. It may often not be the best format for teaching and learning. But when a circle of seating is established, in contrast to the normal seating arrangements, a different kind of conversation is invited forward. This very difference can open up new perspectives and change what gets spoken about and how people speak.

Circles are venues for enhancing connections between people in a frequently fragmented and disconnected world. As traditional family systems continue to change, many young people are not invited to participate in the solving of family problems. They tend to stick to their peer groups and become exposed to a limited range of opinions and ideas. Consequently, they seldom have the chance to listen to divergent opinions about their world.

Circles in schools can serve preventative purposes, as well as being used to respond to trouble of many kinds. They can be used to create a unique class identity, consolidate positive values, and build connections and links that previously were not available. The anthropologist Barbara Myerhoff (1982) believed that communities of people talking together in groups helped form identity narratives for individuals and also for groups of people. Talk in circles defines us as members of a group and structures our relationships with each other. A circle thus provides a "definitional ceremony" where individual, group, or community identities are formed. Myerhoff argued that when people tell stories aloud in groups, the effect on the listener is profound. "The listener is changed," she said (p. 116).

Circle time promotes the development in young people of the value systems that enable democracy to flourish. We shall illustrate its use here through the telling of a story. In this instance, Mike is the storyteller.

A CASE VIGNETTE

"There seems to be something not working with my tutor class," the teacher said over a cup of tea during our morning break.

"Oh," I replied. "What's your guess about what the problem might be?"

"I can't put my finger on it, but there's constant niggling and an undercurrent of tension."

"How does that show itself?" I probed further.

"Well, they take ages to get started on learning tasks, they don't listen to me, they don't contribute to class discussions, they snigger at each other, they come late to class. . . . Is that what you mean?"

"Yes," I answered. "What impact is that having on the students in the class and on you?"

"They don't seem to be happy, and the quiet ones look scared of the others. And how does it affect me? I worry about whether I will be able to achieve results with this class. I know they have potential, but they just can't settle down. It's been 4 weeks. I've been trying to get them to work and all my other classes are going well. I can't understand it. Other teachers of the same class say that there are a lot of putdowns and mocking. There are some students who seem determined to wreck the class."

"I have an idea than might work in this case. I suggest we ask them what is happening and see if they can find some solutions to these problems."

"I've tried that, but they can't give me any answers."

"It may help if we could get the class into a circle and together give them an opportunity to say what's on their minds and think about how to make changes. I will organize the plan and we will work as a team. What do you say?"

She tentatively agreed to this suggestion, and we decided on a time for this circle. She admitted that she had some misgivings, as this was new to her, but she agreed to give it a try.

Establishing the Circle of Relationships

Prior to meeting with the class, I analyzed test results for each student and found a wide range of abilities. They were a diverse mix of cultures, and comments in students' personal files from previous schools revealed many "issues," such as family problems, learning and social difficulties, and discipline matters. I sighed inwardly and said to myself, "No wonder!"

I created the plan below and discussed it with the teacher. The objective of the circle process would be to address conflict in the class and to decide how to change it. Reports from other teachers had mentioned a spate of teasing put-downs, which were preventing many students from learning. A circle would provide a process where all students could have their say about what was happening and about its effects, and solutions could be generated. Students and teachers together would be invited to take responsibility for actions that were transpiring.

The teacher and I decided not to let the students know about the circle in advance. We thought the element of surprise might help ensure its success. As the class filed in, they were surprised to see me in the room. They sat noisily down in their seats. After the teacher had welcomed them and called for attention, I introduced myself and asked the class to quickly and quietly put the desks to one side and form a circle with the chairs. I explained that the teacher and I would be sitting in the circle and there would be no empty seats. Boys and girls were seated alternately around the circle. The purpose of this was to disrupt the possibility of cliques of peers forming power blocs within the conversation.

They asked me what this was about, and I said that I would tell them once we were seated in a circle. The anticipation was palpable, and the teacher was surprised to see how efficiently they completed the task. Then students were introduced to the rules that would govern the circle conversation (see Box 8.1).

BOX 8.1
GUIDELINES FOR CIRCLE CONVERSATION

1. The person is not the problem; the problem is the problem.

2. The person speaking should not be interrupted.

3. Conversation goes around the circle one by one. People are entitled to pass, but it is not preferred.

4. People should signal if they wish to speak.

5. There will be no put-downs.

6. Nobody is to name anyone in a negative way.

7. The most important emphasis is on creating a new story, not rehashing over and over the problem story.

8. What is said in here stays in here.

9. A circle is a form of democracy where everyone is valued and has a right to speak.

10. This is a special and sacred class period. If you can't stick to the rules, you will be excluded and have no rights to be heard. You will have to sit outside the circle.

11. Special hand signals will be used. An open palm means I want to speak. Hands up means that I hear a put-down or I see someone not participating.

I explained the rationale for the circle and discussed the rules for this meeting. I also explained the importance of safety when sharing thoughts and feelings and how, when the circle was over, what was discussed would stay in the room.

Setting the Agenda

Some students said excitedly, "We did this at our last school!"

There was enthusiasm for the circle, and I set out the agenda for our meeting, including reviewing the questions we would discuss and the hoped-for outcomes (see Box 8.2).

BOX 8.2
AGENDA FOR THE CIRCLE CONVERSATION

1. A moment's silence is called for to begin. "The person is not the problem; the problem is the problem" was written on the board.

2. Round 1: What has been making learning hard in this class? No names, just behavior. What have been the effects on you of these things? (Ms. Garcia will write your ideas on the board.)

3. Round 2: What helps to make it easier to learn in this class? Give examples of these things happening.

4. Round 3: What must we do to have the kind of class relationships where we can learn?

5. What are you personally prepared to do to make these things happen? Students write their initials by the actions that they are prepared to do to change things.

6. Round 4: Future plans: Open discussion. Remember to use hand signals. What must we do to cement in these changes? How can teachers help? What follow-up is needed to ensure these commitments are carried forward?

7. Round 5: Review of what everyone thinks of the changes. What difference has been created? When will we hold the next circle? Can we hold a celebration of achievement of peaceful relations when the work discussed here has taken place?

8. Round 6: Praise and acknowledgment round. Students are asked to give some praise or acknowledgment for another student in the class. Everybody must have something positive said about them.

The expectant atmosphere gave me an opportunity to set the conversation in motion.

Addressing the Issues

"What has been making learning hard in this class?" I began. "And I am also interested in hearing what have been the effects of these things on you personally."

This question identifies the problem story of relationships in the class and traces the effects of the problem on each person. Because the relationships in a class are made up of a complex network of interactions, there are likely to be many dimensions to the problem story. All perspectives should be simply accepted, as long as the rules are observed. No one's description of the problem is privileged as better than anyone else's.

Students began to explain the many difficulties they had been experiencing. They were telling each other what lay behind the tension in the class. They talked about what was important to them and how they wanted to be heard.

"I didn't really know anybody when I came, and it's been hard getting to make friends."

"There's so much noise, I can't concentrate."

"People laugh at me when I answer a question."

"Some people are silly and immature."

"I can't trust anyone here."

"There's too much mucking around and the teacher can't get started."

It seemed as if everybody had something to say, and when they had nothing new to add, the students said that it had already been said. The teacher drew three columns on her whiteboard and, after adding her impressions in the circle about what made it hard for her to teach, she stood up and began recording all the students' ideas.

Opening the Counter Story

After everybody had had their say, I introduced the next round.

"What helps to make it easier to learn in this class?"

This question seeks out the counter story of relationships. Under the dominance of the problem story, the counter story will likely be harder to identify at first. So it is necessary to be patient and expect that it will take longer to emerge. There was a period of silence before they started.

"Listening?" said Julia tentatively.

"That's a good start," I said. "Thanks, Julia. Let's just go around in a clockwise direction now."

"Having all our equipment ready."

"Settling down to work as soon as we come in."

"Keeping the noise level down."

"Having fun things to do."

"Lots of activities."

"Everybody cooperating."

"Nice music."

"It's this class, I love coming here, and they all make me feel good."

"It's better if you can trust people."

Some students said that their ideas had already been mentioned, so we passed on to the next person. After everyone had had a chance to contribute, I asked if there was anybody who had noticed anything about themselves during that round. This was a question that invited the class to thicken the small pieces of the counter story previously mentioned. It drew all of the suggestions together and invited the making of meaning around them. In order to establish a counter story as viable and likely to be sustained, such thickening is important.

"I have never thought about this stuff before," Lucas offered. "It's important."

"Thanks, Lucas," I said. Expressing appreciation is preferable to passing judgment by saying, "Good." It invokes a different relationship, which is less about power and more affirming of a person's creativity.

Commitment to Action

"The next round involves considering making a commitment to doing what you can to make a difference each day. I would like each person to say what they will do to make this class the very best class for enjoying learning and getting along with each other. Ms. Garcia will write your name beside your contribution in the middle column and then, when it's finished, she will type up the whole chart, so that you can have your own copy of the action plan for your class. Who would like to start?"

This question is designed to turn suggestions into actions. It also thickens the story further but does so along the landscape of action (White, 2007), rather than along the landscape of meaning. What is being planned is a series of plot developments in the story of class relationships. Each development reverberates around the circle, because everyone gets to hear the plan.

"I will really try to keep my voice down," said Layla. "If others are loud, I will tell them to shush."

"I will listen more to the teacher and not let myself get distracted."

"Come in quieter."

"Stop others from mocking anyone."

"Not respond to other kids making comments."

The teacher carefully wrote down all their ideas, and by the end of the three rounds, her whiteboard contained very rich and detailed information about how the students saw the classroom learning environment, what they preferred, and a clear plan for how it could be achieved.

Documenting students' ideas and circulating them help the ideas to reverberate longer. This turns verbal commitments into written documents, which grants them greater status and legitimacy as not just momentary thoughts but longer-lasting ones. It makes them more likely to be adhered to.

I thanked the students for their contributions and for how well they had stayed focused for the whole period. I told them how impressed I was at their honesty and willingness to create the kind of class that maximizes learning.

"Now I want to ask for your thoughts about solving problems in this way," I said and sat back and waited. There were lots of nervous giggles and students looking unsure.

This question makes another fold in the new story of classroom relationships. Inquiry is now focused on the landscape of meaning. Again the story thickens.

A hand went up.

"I thought we had a pretty good class," Shivneil said. "I didn't realize that there was so much mocking and put-downs. Now that I know, I can do something about it."

"I liked talking like this, in a circle. I don't usually speak much," Ravi said.

"When can we do this again?" Rhonda asked. "It's cool!"

"Let's see how well you can grow the kind of class you and your teacher want, and then maybe you can have a little celebration and invite me. I can bring a cake along and enough juice for everyone!" I said.

"The next and last thing, before we quickly put the class back to how it was, is a 'praise and acknowledgment round.'" I invite each person around the circle to acknowledge and praise another student for how that person makes his or her day a little better.

"I'll start," their teacher said. "I want to acknowledge all the students who see me in the playground and say 'Hi!' to me as I walk around."

"I want to acknowledge Georgina and Layla and Marsha for helping me with my work."

"I want to acknowledge Patrick and Page and Judah for having fun at lunchtime."

"Calvin waits for me before class and we sit down together."

"Rachael calls me up if I am away and tells me what I missed and gives me her notes."

"This is very good acknowledging," I said after everybody had said something positive about their fellow students. "What difference does hearing such acknowledgments make?"

Once more, I was inviting them to make a further fold in the relationship meanings being generated in the class.

"It makes me want to come to school."

"I didn't know that my mates thought that about me."

"I am a better person now. I can help my classmates."

"We should do this again!"

There were many such comments from students as they considered the effects of the discussions.

"Thanks for working together in such a mature way," I said as the bell rang. "Now let's put the chairs and tables back as you go."

The teacher and I met after the class had filed quietly out.

"I must admit I wasn't sure how this would go, Mike, but I am amazed how sincere they were and how honest their responses were. They were engaged in the process from the start, and they all contributed! Some students who never speak in class had something to say. I was impressed at their willingness to take ownership of their behavior and how easily they committed themselves to doing something positive."

Two weeks later, the teacher reported that students in her class were much more engaged in learning. Relationships were more harmonious and mutually supportive. Her subsequent lessons were characterized by students participating well in discussions. There was no laughing when a student answered a question. They came into the classroom in an orderly manner and responded better to questions about their learning. Students took their conduct in the class more seriously, and some thanked the teacher for organizing the circle and for producing good lessons. A number of other teachers from the same department asked for circle conversations in their class and are keen also to conduct the circles themselves.

SUMMARY

This chapter has been about the use of circles to address conflicts bubbling over within a class. Sometimes it is necessary to create enough of a difference for a story of difference to gather momentum. Small differences through teacher correction of the behavior of individuals often do not generate enough change to be sustained. The circle conversation, when it is established properly, changes many things at once. It introduces new information into the system of relationships and constitutes, in Gregory Bateson's (1972) terms, the difference which makes a difference. The circle interrupts the usual patterns of relational dominance and introduces a new ethic into class relations, based on an equalizing of the voices of all class members and an invitation for new perspectives to be voiced. At the same time, the role of the teacher is honored and included. She is in the position of contributor to the conversation but also of listener and scribe for students' knowledge. In this role, she can magnify and extend the influence of important statements. It is a role that corresponds perfectly with the task of facilitating learning.

QUESTIONS FOR REFLECTION

1. Why are ideas that originate in students' thinking more likely to be implemented as changes in classroom relationships than ideas that originate in teachers' thinking?

2. Recall a conversation with a teacher about frustrations with a class. How could the circle time process have addressed the concerns?

3. How could circle time be used in classes for other purposes so that it would be no surprise when it is introduced for conflict resolution?

4. How does circle time as outlined here contribute to the development of democratic citizenship?

QUESTIONS FOR RESEARCH

1. How can improvements in classroom relationships be measured and documented?

2. What is the impact of circle conversations on relationships between students? On academic success? On disciplinary referrals?

3. What democratic principles are exhibited in students who have been exposed to circle time?

4. Develop a case study of the meanings generated by one particular circle conversation.

9

Undercover
Anti-Bullying Teams

WHAT IS BULLYING?

Here is a definition of bullying from a prominent bullying researcher, Dan Olweus (1993):

> A student is being bullied or victimized when he or she is exposed, repeatedly and over time, to negative actions on the part of one or more other students. (p. 9)

Olweus explains further that "negative actions" refers to the intentional infliction of injury or discomfort and includes threatening, teasing, taunting, and name-calling, as well as physical assaults. We may add to this definition by noting that one-off egregious assaults can also be included in the kinds of behaviors that produce an atmosphere of threat.

Bullying is a very common experience of school for too many young people. Olweus (1993) found that it affected 1 in 7 students in Scandinavian schools and cited studies that replicated these figures in other countries. The U.S. Department of Education Institute of Education Sciences (IES) (2007) found a higher figure among students in the 12 to 18 age group: 32% were victims of bullying in the previous school year and of those, 4% were subject to cyber bullying. What's more, 79% of these instances of bullying took place during school. It can happen at any age, from kindergarten to high school, when someone, or a group of someones acting in concert, decides to engage in practices of power and domination in relation to another. Research studies like those cited above suggest that boys and girls are equally likely to be targets of bullying but that bullying of girls is often done by boys and girls acting together. Bullying by girls need not involve physical violence. Indeed, when practiced by girls, there is often little overt physical violence, but there are other, just as powerful, tactics used. Often these practices are referred to as relational aggression (Crick, 1995; Goldstein, Young, & Boyd, 2008; Prinstein, Boerger, & Vernberg, 2001; Underwood, 2003). *Relational aggression* is "behavior that intentionally harms another individual through the manipulation of social relationships" (Goldstein et al., 2008, p. 642). While this term is frequently associated with the bullying of girls, boys can also use these tactics, especially when sanctions for overt violence are strong enough to have a deterrent effect.

Relational aggression can involve repeated teasing, mocking, name-calling, put-downs, social exclusion, and deliberate isolation from friends. It is manifested in behaviors such as greeting someone systematically with a hostile stare or a turned back, spreading rumors or stories, sharing secrets that were not supposed to be shared, excluding someone from groups or parties, "outing" someone as gay or lesbian, or pressuring a person to do—or not to do—something against his or her will (for example, "I won't be your friend if you talk to her"). When a pattern of such behavior targets an individual student, there is little difference in effect from the traditional concept of bullying. A person's right to peace and ordinary relationships with others is violated. Therefore, such relational violations should be taken just as seriously as expressions of physical violence.

Bullying between students often occurs under the radar, so few adults realize it is happening or that it has become as serious as it has. Only 36% of those who were subject to bullying in the IES (2007) study notified a teacher or other adult. Despite the fact that more bullying happens at school than outside it, teachers are often not alert to the seriousness of what is going on because they are more primed to respond to behaviors that directly disrupt their teaching (confirmed by Olweus's 1993 research). Parents, too, are often unaware of the extent to which their children are subject to bullying (Olweus, 1993) because young people are often reluctant to tell them. Many young people, and particularly boys who are bullied, are ashamed that they are not able to stand up for themselves. They also do not want their parents coming steaming down to school and demanding retribution, or worse still, contacting the families of those who are responsible for the bullying. From the student's perspective, such actions could make matters worse. When social networking sites such as Facebook or Twitter are used to bully young people, parents sometimes threaten to remove the computer or take away a mobile phone in order to prevent the bullying. For students, such measures can seem worse than the bullying.

A student who is being bullied may be lucky enough to have a teacher notice and do something about it, but many victims are not so lucky. Bullying can seriously disrupt students' learning and their overall sense of well-being at school without necessarily disrupting class lessons. We believe that schools need to develop active and effective approaches that interrupt the effects of bullying.

STORIES OF BULLYING

In order to get a feel for what bullying is like, it is worth pausing to look at some examples of what can happen. The following examples of bullying behavior are drawn from one secondary school over several years.

1. A student with an artificial limb tells this story:

In most of my classes I am in, I get hit in the head. On the way to most of my classes, kids kick my leg and mock me a lot, saying things like "legless" and other really mean things. In science, people take my stuff, like my pencil case. Sometimes they open it up and tip stuff on the floor or throw it out the window.

2. A student who broke up with a friend tells a story of cruel retaliation:

We broke up as friends but tried to sort it out. A rumor was started by that person about my grandmother being dead. I felt really hurt because the rumor was not true and I love my grandmother.

3. In this example, a student's ability to form a relationship with the opposite sex is made a subject of attack.

In science, this girl wanted to be in my group. Then she started saying that I couldn't get a girlfriend and if I could, it must be a rat. Then she said that she was going to get her humongous boyfriend to beat me up and told me to watch my back.

4. Bullying frequently picks on body characteristics and belittles a person:

I was waiting outside my social studies class and he comes over and tells the girls who were also waiting, "He's too fat to fit in his car." All the girls laughed.

5. Sometimes bullying appears like random violence:

I was walking home and he came along behind me and jumped on my back. I asked him what that was about and he punched me and walked off. It's the same kid who urinated in my bag and on my computer one day.

6. Perpetrators of bullying often play up to an audience:

We were going to my next class when this boy started saying I was vertically challenged, I needed anger management, I was a masturbating midget. I sat down and he came and picked up my books and threw them on the ground. Everyone laughed when I went to pick them up.

7. Sometimes it seems like bullying targets any kind of difference:

Some girls were mocking me. They were laughing at me and making jokes about me. I would just sit in my wheelchair and do nothing, 'cause there's nothing I can do. The teachers do nothing. They know but they don't do anything. People say stuff like, "handicapper" and kids kick the wheelchair. They kick the bottom of my shoe because it's big.

8. It is not uncommon for bullying to focus on homophobic themes:

In English, this kid calls me a faggot and accuses me of looking at him. He just keeps on saying the same thing over and over again. All his mates just laugh and support him.

9. Here is a bullying story in which intimidation becomes petty theft:

She was helping herself to my pens without asking. Then she got all my books. I never say no to her, because I am sure she will wreck all my stuff. She says bad words to me, calling me names and stuff like that. She took my money and I said nothing. She opened my bag and then she got the money out of my bag. She asked me if I had any more money and I told her. She took it and never gave it back.

10. The angry response to bullying can become the target of more teasing:

I am doing my work and then one of them tells that people hate me. They always talk about me and what I have done wrong. They call me volcano and say that I am about to explode. Some people take my ruler and pens and throw them on the roof.

These examples are reminders of how mean people can be to each other. These behaviors all have serious consequences for the person on the receiving end. Sometimes this person does retaliate and make matters worse, but we need to make clear distinctions between practices of power and clumsy practices of resistance to such power. They are not the same.

Lest we be mistaken, let us list some of the effects of these examples of bullying reported by the person targeted as the victim.

1. It makes me not want to do my schoolwork and I don't talk with my friends and family. When my mum sees that I am upset, she starts crying. When my dad gets home and my mum tells him what's wrong, he gets angry at the bullies and has hit the wall with his fist.

2. My mum has noticed how quiet I am and I have thought about hurting myself but I don't want to give anybody any satisfaction that they have hurt me.

3. I was pretty upset and shaking a little bit and then I started to bring up tears, which I had to hold back, because I didn't want her to see that I was nearly crying. If I let others see how they had affected me, they would have made my life a whole lot worse.

4. I am not happy and I want to go home. I can't pay attention properly, because I can't stop thinking about what people are saying. Teachers think I am struggling. It's because of all this stuff that's going on around me.

5. I felt really upset and want to go home and never come back. I wanted to stab the bully for a couple of seconds. I really hated him. It makes me feel useless, because they call me "dumb blonde." I feel powerless all the time and I feel like not many people support me at the moment.

6. I have thoughts about going to another school. I've thought about retaliating but I've never built up the courage. I am a shy person. I can't do anything to stop him and so I just leave it. There is no way I can get them in trouble because the rest of the class support him and say he didn't do anything. I am sick of it.

7. I tried to keep a smile on my face but, when I get home, sometimes I can't stop crying. I didn't tell my parents, because I felt stupid, but now I have told them.

8. My mum knows about this teasing and has told me to ignore it. Well, that doesn't help, because they don't stop, they just keep going. Teachers don't seem to care. They just carry on teaching. I want to run away from home and school. It does no good telling my parents.

9. I feel like a crazy person, because I am trying hard not to lash out.

One question that needs to be asked when judging the difference between bullying and retaliation is whether both actions produce these kinds of effects. Often such effects are sought out and even enjoyed by those who perpetrate the bullying as they bask in the glow of their power. The same is not usually true when a victim retaliates.

COMMON APPROACHES TO BULLYING

One student was asked what she had tried doing about the bullying. In response, she told a familiar story.

"Everybody has told me to do all these things like fight back or ignore them, but nothing I've ever tried has worked and it has only made things worse! I think I just have to take it."

In spite of widespread concern over the effects of bullying and many initiatives by policy makers worldwide, still the most common advice that is given to people who are being bullied is, "Just learn how to handle it! It will go away." Parents who have experienced bullying themselves at school will often tell their children how they had to learn to live with it. "And so should you," they say.

The problem is that this seldom works. Perpetrators of bullying can easily see that their efforts are striking home, even on the person who tries to ignore it, and they are encouraged to keep on doing it. Having an effect and enjoying the sense of power is what sustains bullying. Seeing someone trying to tough it out and ignore the problem can be a source of amusement, and the bullying effort is just intensified to see how long the target can last before he or she cracks and reacts with some outburst.

The other common approach advocated by many is to get tough and fight back. There are many stories in the movies and in folk psychology of how the victim took up bodybuilding, or learned karate, or formed his or her own gang and came back to fight the bully and win. There is, however, a real danger of the victim becoming just another bully. Or the bullying behavior can simply escalate to more dangerous forms of violence.

Another common, but perhaps surprising, response to bullying is to blame the victim. When someone complains about being bullied, the person is often asked what she or he has been doing to provoke the bullying, as if that explained why it is happening. Some students attract reputations in schools for being victims. Even in situations where evidence can be found for this narrative of victims provoking others into angry responses, those doing the bullying do not have to continue to violate the person being bullied. Blaming the victim seldom produces changes in the incidence of the bullying.

What is needed is a more systematic approach in which schools take bullying seriously and actively work to counter it. Systematic playground supervision is known to decrease instances of bullying. So too are deliberate schoolwide programs to reduce bullying, using class lessons, class conferences, teacher awareness campaigns, systematic sanctions, and parent involvement (Olweus, 1993).

The most common official response is to identify the bully, isolate the individual offender, and mete out punishment. Punishment, however, may inhibit the problem without really addressing it. It also potentially sends out the wrong moral message. The implicit message is that the power of the school authorities is stronger than the power of the bully and therefore must prevail. Bullying is addressed primarily by overpowering it. The trouble is that this message mimics the same message that is contained in the bullying practices. Moreover, it is not an empowering message for either victims or perpetrators. The ball is taken out of their hands.

There are also the side effects of punishment to consider. Punishment can produce simmering resentment, which can all too easily come back on the target if this person has complained to a teacher. Retribution against those who complain of bullying is all too common. Victims often know this well and are, therefore, unwilling to come forward in situations where their suffering is quite intense. Another side effect of punishment can be a shaming of the perpetrator that has negative consequences for that person's development. It may actually increase the likelihood that, out of such shame, the person becomes more inclined to repeat the bullying behavior on someone else.

We do not want to suggest that a retributive model (Zehr, 1990, 2002) of responding to bullying with strong punishments is always wrong or that there are not circumstances where it is necessary. But we are interested in exploring other methods that might prove effective in transforming behavior and relationships among students. That is what this chapter aims to address.

Individual counseling of victims or perpetrators does not necessarily work either. Bullying is the kind of relational problem with which school counselors should be ready to deal, but the supportive nature of personal counseling often does not provide sufficient challenge to bring about significant changes in behavior for perpetrators. For good reasons, the work of school counselors has been distanced from the administrative role of disciplinary management. The contribution that counselors can make to managing troublesome behavior has been understood as producing role conflict with their supportive role of helping students deal with personal and social-emotional problems. As we saw in Chapter 5, new forms of restorative practice work for counselors are being imagined that reintroduce them into the sphere of discipline in schools, not so much as authority figures but as process managers. When school principals and school counselors both understand these new roles, they can make the processes work without creating role conflict.

UNDERCOVER ANTI-BULLYING TEAMS

Establishing undercover anti-bullying teams is an example of a practice that breaks new ground for counselors and employs their professional skills in a way that addresses behavior problems and transforms relationships, without resorting to an authoritarian approach. It can reduce bullying in a school to the benefit of students' learning, teachers' classroom management, and administrators' workloads. The term "undercover teams" was coined by Bill Hubbard (2004) drawing on a "no blame" approach to bullying, after Robinson and Maines (1977). We have elaborated it in two further articles that those interested in taking up this approach would be wise to study (Williams, 2010; Williams & Winslade, 2008). We shall explain here the concept of the undercover anti-bullying team and illustrate it with a case vignette.

The practice outlined here draws from a narrative perspective that understands the practice of bullying as a narrative performance. Perpetrators, targets, and bystanders act out their roles along a known plot trajectory. Each is a participant in a problematic storyline, rather than a problem person in her or his essence. To repeat the refrain from earlier chapters, "The person is not the problem; the problem is the problem." Or in this case, "The bully is not the problem, the bullying is the problem!"

We also do not want to totalize individuals' identities (Winslade & Monk, 2007) as "bullies" or "victims." Instead, we assume that every person involved in the bullying relationship is also capable of other styles of relationship. No one is a bully or a victim by nature. The bully, the victim, and the bystander are names, not so much of persons as of positions in a narrative. People enter these positions and perform their narrative function, but they can also set the story aside, given an effective invitation to do so. The challenge is to create an opportunity for each of them to step out of the story of bullying and into another storyline that is incompatible with ongoing bullying.

The bullying relationship is more central to the practice of bullying than the personal identity of either the bully or the victim. Hence, it makes sense to target the bullying relationship directly for transformation. The undercover teams approach does just this. It is best explained through telling a story of this approach in action.

A CASE VIGNETTE

"There's a student in my year 9 [equivalent to Grade 8 in the United States] class who is getting picked on by a number of her classmates," the teacher said, as he sat down beside me.

"I have tried to stop them by shifting them around and telling them off, but I still see her crying sometimes and she won't tell me what is wrong. I am worried about her. She doesn't work and just sits there. Would you see Judith, please?" he asked.

I agreed and called Judith out of her class. When she arrived at my office, I explained that her teacher had seen her crying and suspected that someone was being mean to her. I asked her gently if this was happening and she nodded. She looked embarrassed but said that she was being bullied. I told her that I was really interested in hearing about it because I have been developing a special program to banish bully-ing that works well. She seemed a little suspicious and may have heard all this before.

"Before I decide whether this program would work, I would like to hear your story. I would like also to write it down. I will check with you as we go to make sure that I get it right."

I paused for a while.

"If I think my special program would work for you, I would need to get this story correct, because I would need to use it. Is that okay by you?"

Judith agreed and I took out a form and began to record her story.

"All my life I've been bullied. People tease me about my red hair and because I'm small. Somebody even said I was so small I couldn't read, but basically they've been teasing me about my hair. They make my life hard by making rude comments about me. They call me 'fanta pants' and 'ginga girl' and even 'carrot midget.' I hate that. This morning I heard some kids making up a song about me.

"'Why was she born? How can she still be alive? Whenever I look at her my own eyes will crack,' they were singing.

"I get questions about why I dye my hair but I don't. They say I should dye my hair blue or blonde or brown, anything but red hair. I can't help my hair. My granddad says it's what makes me special!"

I asked her, "How does the bullying affect you?"

"It makes me feel sad, angry, hurt, small. It makes me wonder what's happened to them to make them bully me and why they don't bully other people. I want to punch people, throw things, I feel like hitting my sister and kicking her in the shins. I can't stop crying when people bully me. I am a kind of crybaby, that's what my sister calls me. She's six and she's deaf and she calls _me_ a crybaby. It also gets me to write mean things about them in my book that I don't really mean. I yell at my family and slam doors. I shout. I throw my toys around my room and that gets me into trouble with Mum. Sometimes my friends are affected. I take it out on them."

I asked her how she would prefer things to be. She thought for a while, then said with a smile on her face, "Cheerful, everybody getting along, everybody being friends. That way I can be happy at home, not yell or get my mouth washed out with soap (just a threat, it has not happened yet). I just want to be enjoying life."

"I am pretty sure that we can get rid of this bullying for you," I said. "You won't have to do a thing to change, but I would like you to notice every change that occurs," I said.

"That's great," she replied.

The first step in establishing an undercover anti-bullying team is for the counselor to meet with the target of the bullying, listen carefully to the story of what has been happening, and ascertain whether or not an instance of bullying has taken place. If it has, then the counselor introduces the idea of setting up an undercover team. The counselor should describe the undercover team as a covert operation in which some secrecy is needed for it to succeed. It is referred to as something like a "Mission Impossible" project. The sense of intrigue makes the setting up of the undercover team into a playful approach, which often adds to its appeal. Children and young people are often irresistibly drawn to what Freeman, Epston, and Lobovits (1997) call "playful approaches to serious problems."

"What may work in your case," I said to Judith, "is an undercover team, made up of students that you and I and your teachers select, with the number one purpose of getting rid of the bullying. Each team includes the two students who are doing the worst bullying and four or five others that the rest of the class respect. It's better if we can get a mix of girls and boys. The reason we include the ones doing the bullying is that I have found that those students often bully because they have an audience and they need to learn how to be supportive. The others on the team seem to teach them how to do that.

"The thing that makes these teams work is that they are like secret agents, working 'under cover' to seek out bullying and to do whatever they can to stop it. I can show you many real-life examples of how they have worked for other students, if you like.

"When they are all together, I tell them they have been specially selected by you and their teachers to be an undercover team: secret agents whose job is to eliminate bullying in their class. I would like to read out your bullying story to them, so that they get a clear idea of what it's been like for you. I will not use any names, because we don't want anybody getting their revenge back on you. I just want them to hear a true story of bullying. What do you think?"

"I suppose," she said cautiously.

In the second step of the process, the counselor invites the victim to select six people to be members of the undercover team. Included among those six are two of the worst perpetrators of the bullying. The other members can be made up of boys and girls who have never, as far as the target knows, been victims of bullying and have never bullied others. They should be students whom others might look up to as respected classmates. It is wise to check with a teacher, especially if the victim of the bullying cannot easily identify these team members.

The third step is for the counselor to meet with the chosen team and convey the information that a member of their class has been harassed and bullied. The counselor reads them a condensed version of the story of the bullying and outlines a brief list of its effects, drawing directly on the words of the target but without naming anyone. The counselor then asks the team members to respond to this story. They often express shock or outrage at what is happening. Then the counselor invites them to be part of a special covert operation that nobody knows about, working in secret to support the victim and help this person through a difficult time. They are not asked to be the person's friend, but just to be friendly to him or her. The counselor emphasizes several times that this is strictly a secret team and that nobody must know of its existence. The counselor goes on to explain that, upon the successful conclusion of the team, that is, when the bullying has stopped, they will be awarded a food voucher (or other suitable reward) and will receive a principal's award. The inclusion of the principal's award grants a certain legitimacy to the covert operation.

The counselor only reveals the name of the target after all of the students have agreed to be part of the team (even though some may have guessed). The counselor then asks the undercover team to develop a detailed plan for how they will get the bullying to stop and how they will create a different experience of school for the victim. Once a plan is formed, the counselor asks the team members to discuss how to carry it out covertly.

I printed off a list of Judith's class, and we talked about who would best be able to eliminate the bullying. We discussed each student in turn and, once we had identified the two who were responsible for most of the bullying, we focused on selecting students who, as far as Judith could tell, didn't bully and seemed not to have been bullied themselves. These were the students others looked up to. I explained that I would share this list with her teachers and ask for their input.

When I had organized her undercover team and they had a plan to eliminate the bullying, I would call her back and check on progress. It would be up to her to say when the bullying had stopped.

Before she returned to class, I reminded her to keep the undercover team idea secret, because the team needs to make changes in their own time and in their own way. We agreed that the best way of getting rid of bullying is to enable the bullies to learn new ways to relate to others, not because they have been forced to by the school authorities, but because of their own choice to do so.

I e-mailed her teachers after school with the following message:

> *Hi, Teachers,*
>
> *Judith . . . has told me a story about some bullying of the continual teasing, name-calling, mocking family, type. Others might think of it as "low level," but to her it's big and causing her to switch off school. Some of you may have seen the effects it's having on her as well. Judith and I think that an undercover team might work well to eliminate the bullying.*
>
> *She has selected the following as members of the team: Brendon, Rajal, Janet, Bernadine, Rewi, George, and Nico. These are the students she wants to support her. This group includes the two "worst bullies."*
>
> *Considering what you know about these students, can you suggest any others that may be more suitable or any concerns about those on this list?*
>
> *If you think this is a reasonably good team to work undercover in secret, searching out bullying when they see it and getting rid of it, there is no need to reply. I need to call the team together tomorrow, so would appreciate your prompt feedback.*
>
> *On the side of a bullying-free school,*
> *Mike*

I invited each student on the team to a meeting in my office during lunch break but gave no indication of the purpose of the meeting, and no student knew that the others had been called up.

When they began to drift in, they were all asking what this was about and were surprised to see the two bullying students with them. I had my room set up with the seats in a circle, and those two boys looked very uncertain. When I motioned for them all to sit down, I made sure that they didn't sit together but seated them alongside others in the circle, being careful to ignore their obvious discomfort.

I explained that they had all been specially selected to do a job that nobody else could do. They looked at each other, wondering what this could be about.

With a serious look of concern on my face, I said, "There's some bullying going on in your class and it's affecting one student in particular. Your teacher noticed her crying in class and asked if I could help. I spoke to this student and she told me a story of some pretty bad bullying. I suggested to her that the best people to eliminate this bullying are the students in her class, and she agreed.

"You are here because she selected you to be on a special secret team with the difficult task of bringing peace and harmony back and eliminating her bullying forever. Your teachers have agreed with her selection.

"It will be up to her to say when the bullying has gone and, if this team is successful, you will all get a food voucher and a principal's certificate in recognition for your work in making our school free of bullying. Are you up to that? Can you keep a secret?"

Predictably, there were a number of reactions at this time. Some bullies will confess; others will try to shift the blame onto others in the class. They will often go very quiet. Sometimes they will deny their involvement. Even if they are quiet, they usually warm to the idea, once the other students start talking about their plan for changing the classroom relationships. I have never had a team where a student doesn't want to get involved.

At this point, I say, "You may have noticed that I am not interested in blaming anyone. I haven't mentioned any students' names because this story I am going to read is about bullying, not about a bully. Even when students tell me the names of the persons who have been bullying the most, I never tell the team their names, because I believe that the problem is the bullying. Sometimes people are sick of bullying but they don't know how to stop doing it. Are you ready to hear the story now?" I ask.

I read out the story just as it was told to me, including how it had affected Judith and what she would like to happen.

Reactions after hearing the story are typically varied. Some students have cried as they take in the impact of the words; others look around furtively. Those who are the worst bullies are probably waiting to hear their name. Often the others will look over at the bullying students with accusatory looks, but I am careful not to attribute blame to anyone in the room or allow others to do so.

"Now that you have heard Judith's story, we need to develop a five-point plan to get rid of the bullying. Remember that she has personally chosen you, because she knows you to be students with influence in the class. Your teachers know that you have been asked to be on this team, so they too will be looking at how well this undercover team works in getting rid of bullying. One way to get started is to think about what you would like if you were her."

"We could stick up for her when people mock her," said one student.

"Who else would like to do that?" I asked, and as others volunteered, I wrote their names down on the form on which the story of the bullying had previously been recorded.

"We could sit somewhere close to her to stop people mocking her," Rajal offered.

"Say hi to her. Be friendly rather than ignore her," said one and they all nodded. On the form I wrote *All the team*.

"Include her in games and conversations," a couple of girls offered, and I wrote down their names.

"Not leave her out, make friends with her, just talk to her." The whole team nodded and I wrote down *Whole team*.

"Thanks," I said. "That looks like a pretty good plan. There are still a couple of things we need to talk about. How can you keep your work a secret? What are you going to say when other kids notice that the bullying is going away?"

They thought for a while, and then Bernadine said, "We will just say that the guidance counselor has asked us how we are getting on with our work."

"We could have a secret sign when we are doing some anti-bullying stuff," said one girl.

"We could have names for each other," another student offered. They were getting quite excited now.

I thanked them warmly for agreeing to be part of this special mission and said that I would call them back after 5 days of undercover bullying work. I told them I would check with Judith to see if she had noticed any changes. They all left in a positive frame of mind, eager to begin their work.

After a few days, the counselor meets with the victim and asks how things are going. Next, the counselor meets again with the team to review how the plan is working from their perspective. At this point, refinements to the plan sometimes need to be discussed and its effects can be studied. There are, of course, some variations in how the plan works out. Sometimes the cover is blown. Sometimes the perpetrators of the bullying own up to their actions; sometimes they do not. Sometimes the target wants to meet with the undercover team and thank them; on other occasions, this is not necessary.

The undercover teams approach to anti-bullying work is founded on a carefully designed process (see Box 9.1).

BOX 9.1
CALENDAR OF EVENTS FOR AN UNDERCOVER TEAM

Day 1. Interview the target by himself/herself (30 minutes).

Day 2. Assemble the undercover team, explain their mission, and complete the five-point plan (30 min). Inform teachers of the class by e-mail of the existence and purpose of the team.

Day 5. Check with the target to establish progress (10 min). Check with the teachers to confirm progress.

Day 7. Meet the undercover team to check their progress and give encouragement (10–15 min).

Day 9. Meet the target to check again on progress and find out whether bullying has stopped (10 min).

Day 14. When the bullying has stopped, meet the undercover team again to give out certificates, vouchers, and evaluation forms, and plan for the long term (30 min).

Two days later, a smiling Judith came in to see me.

I asked, "How's the class now?"

Her face lit up. "Excellent . . . good . . . superb," she said. "The bullying has stopped and I am so happy. The two bullies have stopped bullying me and they've told their friends, which is good. But I think we should give it a bit longer, just to make sure."

"Thanks for that. I agree that it's early still, and your undercover team has only just begun, but it's a good start," I said and sent her back to class.

Two days later, I called the team together for their next meeting.

"How is the five-point plan going?" I asked.

"It's pretty easy," one boy said. "It's just basic things like saying 'hi' and telling others, 'Don't be sad.'"

One boy said, "I tried being friendly. It worked, kind of."

"Saying 'hi' to her involved her," one girl offered.

"She *has* changed, not too snappy," said another.

"Seems to me like the teacher is picking on her," one student observed.

"Any other changes you have noticed?" I asked when there was a lull in the conversation.

"The change has been that, if you're friendly to her, she is friendly to us!" Brendon said. "It hasn't gone for good yet though. It's also because she does stuff. She snapped at Ariana for no reason."

"Are there any suggestions that you could make that might help her?" I asked.

"Well," Brendon said, "think before you act. That will help her understand that she shouldn't overreact, because she can be annoying."

"We leave her alone now, we don't say stuff. She's quieter now."

I e-mailed Judith's teachers and asked if they had noticed any changes. The English teacher reported that the boy who, for Judith, had been the worst bully was "a model student." Others who replied said that the class atmosphere had improved a lot.

A couple of days later, I called Judith back to see me.

"They can get their stuff now!" she said excitedly. "It's stopped for good and I am so happy! I am sure it's gone long term. My relationship with Janet is way better as well."

"That's so cool!" I said. "Are you sure?"

"Yes, the bullying has stopped and I have even stopped being annoying."

She offered this without any prompting. I smiled because I knew that something positive was taking place.

"On that matter," I began cautiously, "some of the team wondered if you could 'not overreact.' I don't know exactly what they mean, but I suspect that you do," I remarked.

"Oh yes, I know what they mean," she smiled. "One of the team members told me that, and that's made a bi-i-i-i-g difference when I took off my sensitives."

This was teenage speak but I got the message. I sent her back to class and arranged to see the principal to ask him to sign six certificates for this successful team.

The next day, I called in the team to present them with their vouchers and certificates and to have them complete an evaluation form.

They were all smiling and laughing as they filed in to my office and sat in the same seats that they had before.

"This could be the final meeting of this team," I began. "I would like to hear how your mission has gone and whether or not you think that the bullying has disappeared for good. Judith says the bullying has gone and that she's much happier. I reckon it's time to give out the food vouchers and the principal's certificate. What do you think?"

"It's starting to go for good," Rewi said.

"It's good doing the right thing," another said.

"It's a good experience so we know what to do next," another said.

"We did well," Rajal said and they all gave each other a high five.

"If Judith says it's gone, and you say it's gone, then that's good enough for me!" I said enthusiastically.

I gave them each their voucher, evaluation form, and their certificate. As they drifted out, they left me thinking that this was another example of a successful team where students had learned much about each other and the power of doing good for each other.

A SOCIAL LEARNING EXERCISE

What we have illustrated is a strategic intervention into a set of bullying relations. You could say that it directly addresses the social relations of bullying, rather than the psychological motivations for it. Or you can work from the assumptions of social constructionism and attribute psychological responses to what happens between people. It was Lev Vygotsky who famously attributed learning to the process of internalizing what happens in interaction with others. We believe that this process of intervention in bullying relations is indeed a social learning exercise.

As discussed in Chapter 5, Vygotsky (1978, 1986) developed a theory of learning that was about movement through the "zone of proximal development," in which students learn something new they could not master on their own without some help from teachers or other students with more advanced skills in solving problems. As Michael White (2007) shows, this process is as useful for identity development as it is for learning to read. White talks about moving from "what is known and familiar" through the zone of proximal development to what is "possible to know" (p. 277).

Undercover teams provide an opportunity for students to step out of the constraints of their "known and familiar" reputation by trying out ways of relating that have been denied them by the strength and power of the bullying narrative. They are able to expand their relational repertoire to include new behaviors with the help of the "scaffolding" (White, 2007) provided by the other team members and by the school counselor's invitations. In the process, it becomes "possible to know" about their own actions of either bullying or bystanding in a new way and to reflect on the consequences and effects of those bullying behaviors. A young person's capacity for collaboration increases as he or she collaborates with the team members.

Team members hear the story of the bullying and are invited to cross the zone of proximal development in order to collaborate with their peers and to devise an action plan that is specially intended to target the very behaviors that had produced the story of bullying. During the monitoring process, a relational shift occurs when they work together on a common problem, sharing their individual success and giving examples of positive actions. The students whom others may have seen as "innocent bystanders" realize that their inaction in preventing something that they would be morally opposed to, if they thought about it more thoroughly, has actually made it easier for the bullying to survive and flourish. They also learn to move from what is "known and familiar" to what is "possible to know."

The formation of the team and the carrying out of its mission can also be described in terms of a "re-grading ritual" (Epston, 2008). Young people are invited to undertake an act of moral redefinition in relation to the bullying. This is achieved without a shaming process, which might isolate the bullies as shameful and reprehensible but leave the bystander witnessing untouched. At the same time, these teams provide the bullies with a means to reidentify themselves as competent members of a moral community (the rest of the class) that may have been previously denied them. Through the creation of a five-point plan, and in the operation of the plan, the process provides a "test" whereby those responsible for the bullying can make a moral decision between two available identities, that is, between the identities of a caring supporter or a bully.

This particular test bypasses attempts to apportion blame but addresses a more important concern: How durable or how fixed is the bullying relation? The team is a moral community convened for a moral purpose. It provides a space for bullies to test or try out their caring abilities. The trialing of these caring abilities is assessed by the victim, the other team members, teachers, and any parents who are alerted to demonstrations of caring. Their feedback, throughout the monitoring process of the team's life, provides a type of formative assessment for those who are trying to reconstruct an alternative to their bullying reputation.

The process is also founded on a relationship of trust between the school counselor and the principal, who grants his or her sanction to the process through the awarding of a principal's certificate. In this way, the authority of the school is brought to bear in support of a learning process, rather than a punitive one, and the counselor's role is not set up in opposition to the disciplinary authority of the school.

In order to assist the buy-in of those recruited for the team, it is useful to draw upon the archives of previous undercover teams. We have yet to meet a bully who hasn't taken up the challenge. The archive enables the counselor to say, "I have an idea that has worked 25 times before today."

When parents have the purpose and process of the undercover teams carefully explained, most are supportive and are usually surprised that their child has been suffering in silence. In a recent case, a boy was teased because of a large mole on his face. When his parents were made aware of the level of distress this was causing their son, they arranged for the mole to be removed. Together with the efforts of an undercover team, the parents' action brought about dramatic changes for this boy.

SUMMARY

In this chapter, we began by describing bullying and relational aggression as acts of power and domination by one or more students against another student. It is an alarmingly common experience for too many students in schools and takes many forms, not all of which involve physical violation. We outlined some common approaches to bullying, such as encouraging students to ignore it, or punishment-oriented responses, and explained why these are often ineffective. Then we explained the undercover anti-bullying team concept and how it works directly with the relationships involved in the bullying narrative. Through a case vignette, we illustrated how it invites groups of students, including those involved in doing the bullying, to transform the experience of another student at school. The process for establishing an undercover team was explained, and the reasons for its consistent success rate were explored.

QUESTIONS FOR REFLECTION

1. Think about instances of relational aggression and bullying. How might the undercover team approach have worked in these situations?

2. What role does the "undercover" intrigue play in the success of the undercover team approach, and how would you ensure the anonymity of the team?

3. How can school administrators and counselors collaborate to make undercover teams work?

4. What adaptations would you need to make to implement an undercover team in an elementary school, a middle school, or a single-sex school?

5. When might it be useful to include parents in contributing to or being informed about the story of bullying and the story of the undercover team?

6. Why might it be important to carefully document every step in the process and to accurately record the student's verbatim description of the bullying event?

QUESTIONS FOR RESEARCH

1. What forms of bullying and relational aggression occur frequently in your school?

2. How can the effects of bullying and relational aggression on individual students be documented?

3. How can the effects of establishing an undercover team be tracked over time?

4. What are the implementation challenges of establishing the use of undercover teams in a school?

5. What can be learned from developing a case study of the work of one undercover team?

10

Guidance Lessons

GUIDANCE LESSONS TO RAISE CONSCIOUSNESS ABOUT OPPRESSIVE PRACTICES

In the cause of conflict resolution and violence reduction, it is sometimes possible to identify a general pattern of problems occurring in a school. For example, where there are diverse cultural or ethnic groups, tension between these groups can occur as a result of expressions of racism. Or a pattern of low-level harassment of girls by boys can develop as an expression of pervasive patriarchal discourses. Or the presence of a special education unit within the school that caters to a particular form of disability (for example, blindness, deafness, cerebral palsy, or motor disability) can be accompanied by pervasive and prejudiced teasing and name-calling. Or the presence in the school of young people who are openly gay or lesbian or transgendered may trigger prejudiced responses by students, parents, or even teachers. In such circumstances, there is a place for the design of specific lessons aimed at addressing these issues and challenging the discourse that is supporting frequent problems. In many places, school administrators are actually accountable for providing a safe physical and emotional environment for students. This includes providing an environment that is free from prejudice and discrimination on any basis. Hence, these lessons can be seen as part of the basic responsibility of schools to create a hospitable learning environment.

Sometimes a concern may not even be recognized by the victims of the problematic behavior as anything other than an isolated occurrence, simply because it has become a behavioral norm. Everyone has come to think that this is just how things are and has adjusted to the presence of "annoying" behavior without seeing the pervasive pattern. Young people especially may instinctively know that something is hurtful without having developed a clear rationale that links it with a social pattern of injustice. In this case, what is needed is general consciousness-raising, or as Paolo Freire (1970) called it, *conscientization*. Again, this work can be accomplished by the design of specific lessons aimed at addressing the general consciousness about an issue.

Another concept that can be called upon in conceptualizing the purpose of such lessons is Jacques Derrida's (1976) term, *deconstruction*, as discussed in Chapter 2. Contrary to some interpretations, Derrida did not use this term to refer to some kind of destructive activity, like pulling things apart. It is about opening meanings up to scrutiny from some new angle so that surplus, or new meanings, can be released. These new meanings often lie hidden or masked by a narrow range of dominant meanings. Derrida spoke about how the deconstructive impulse often already lies within a field of meanings waiting to be opened up. Deconstruction of powerful lines of force (Deleuze, 1988; Winslade, 2009) that cut across a social field and produce injustice is a laudable goal of guidance lessons.

Such consciousness-raising can certainly take place in the activities discussed elsewhere in this book. Circle conversations can include the deconstruction of dominant discourses. Group counseling can include psycho-educational material that invites group members to unravel dominant assumptions. Restorative conferences and mediations can unpack the discursive material that lies in the background of a particular conflict. And individual counseling can include the externalization of the assumptions drawn from pervasive discourses and internalized into persons. But it is surely economical of professional time to address pervasive issues with whole classes, year groups, and even a whole school, rather than dealing only with every outbreak that arises from the expression of an underlying discourse. General targeted lessons can then later be referred back to in small-group or one-to-one conversations. These lessons can also encourage students to seek help with issues that have arisen during these lessons. The counselor may contribute indirectly as a consultant to these lessons or may actually teach them.

The question for school administrators is about just what sorts of injustice are being perpetuated in a school as an expression of some dominant discourse. Addressing such issues, we would suggest, is of such importance for the development of young people into responsible citizens that it should never be crowded out by an emphasis on other academic subjects. Wise school administrators should use their school counselors to help identify just where, in practice, the pressure points are in a school community. It is all very well to address pervasive social issues of injustice, but the specific expressions of a discourse that are taking place within a school right under the noses of school staff can be completely missed by lessons that do not take account of the particular experiences of the young people most affected by that discourse. Effective change needs to be clearly targeted to students' lived experience, rather than to what adults assume that experience to be. Hence, there needs to be a strong component of listening in identifying the focus of these guidance lessons. We consider this to be a role of the school counselor—to listen to the precise formulation of a discourse in a particular school. This "listening" can be achieved in many ways: regular formal meetings with student leaders, careful analysis of statistical data, and regular meetings with other counselors who have themselves identified "trends."

For example, patriarchal and sexist attitudes toward gender relations may be expressed in an outbreak of a fad of "bra-pinging," as happened in one school. Many boys were collectively expressing the objectification of women through taking pleasure in coming up behind girls in class and pulling their bra straps (through the girls' tops) and letting them go to "ping" against the girl's back. When the girls individually expressed annoyance to the boys at this practice, they were laughed at and advised to learn to "take a joke."

We are using the term *guidance lessons* here for convenience. The kinds of lessons we have in mind might often better be delivered under another heading. In some schools, they may be referred to as health lessons. In others, they may come under social studies. Or they may be picked up by English teachers in relation to literature studies. It matters little what they are called. But we shall refer to them here as guidance lessons, on the assumption that guidance counselors are charged with facilitating the social and emotional development of students in the widest sense, and not just with the individual counseling of those who are suffering or in trouble. Counselors should see their role as sensing the "heartbeat" of the school.

NARRATIVE PRINCIPLES OF GUIDANCE LESSONS

To remain consistent with the principles that have guided the rest of this book, we assume that the pervasive lines of force that channel relationships between people in schools into particular formats are best thought of as socially constructed narratives, rather than hardwired features of human nature. Take racism as an example. It is not something that has always been around (and hence need not be around forever) but was produced as a specific discourse to express the ambition of Europeans to exert dominance over nonwhite peoples during the period of 18th- and 19th-century colonial expansion. Through the process of decolonization, which began as soon as widespread European colonization started, there has been a steady movement to deconstruct the narrative of European "superiority." But elements of the discourse out of which this narrative emerged still remain in the consciousness of both white and nonwhite people, despite the enormous achievements of things such as the civil rights movement. As people perform meaning around these discourse elements, narratives of conflict, complete with their own idiosyncratic plotlines, can occur in schools.

To stress that these are narratives produced out of dominant discourse reminds us that they can be challenged and altered. If they were expressions of human nature, this would be more difficult. It follows that narrative guidance lessons will aim to be respectful of persons, rather than seeking to pathologize them or blame them. The principle that "The person is not the problem; the problem is the problem" will remain paramount. Speaking in externalizing ways about problem issues can be easily translated from counseling and mediation practices into teaching ones. Care will be taken, for example, to talk about racist *assumptions* (which might whisper compellingly in the ear of some people), rather than racist *persons*.

Another assumption these guidance lessons make is that there are always multiple narratives available. In the shadows of a dominating story, there will always be other stories that exist. There will always be some sort of response to the conflict that is also being expressed, perhaps even as a refusal to allow things to get worse. There will often be active resistance on the part of victims. Even if this resistance fails to stop expressions of a dominant discourse, its presence is important and deserves to be honored. The aim of a narrative guidance lesson will be to bring these stories into the light, to invite their articulation more fully, and to magnify them so that they stand a better chance of being chosen as the story of preference.

It is critical, however, that this alternative story emerge from the knowledge of students, particularly those who are victims of the discursive lines of force. It is less empowering for this alternative story to be decided upon by school authorities and promoted by teachers. At best, such an approach is less willingly accepted by the student body. At worst, it is seen as irrelevant, because it does not address the particularities of the problem as it is being performed in the local school context. To allow such local knowledge to emerge and to be included in the building of an alternative story, careful listening and direct questioning is needed.

The exact expressions used within the student discourse repertoire need to be identified, listened to, and carefully recorded, so they can be used as part of the preferred story.

For example, in one school a feud had developed between two groups of students. As the conflict story was told and its effects examined, the desire emerged among a significant number of students for a different kind of relationship with the other group. It was difficult to identify the exact term to describe this relationship ethic because the students were adamant that they did not want to be friends with this group. But they also did not want to continue being enemies. If school authorities insist that students become "friends" as a result of mediation, students may not want to participate, especially if they think that the outcome is preconceived. So they were asked what kind of relationship they would prefer in order for them to get along together. The expression that emerged and gained popularity was that they would remain "neutrals," neither friends nor enemies. In another school, this kind of relationship was referred to as "hi-bye" friends. A clear ethic developed about what it meant to be a neutral, which was quite specific to this conflict situation. It was effective because it was an idea that some students had and could speak to. It was not imposed from above by school authorities. But it could be amplified and given recognition within the school, so that it stood as a counter story to the conflict story that had been feeding the ongoing feud. Ironically, it wasn't long before the "hi-bye" friends became full friends as they let go of the conflict storyline.

INTERVIEWING THE PROBLEM

We are not going to include here a large range of lesson materials for use in lessons built on the principles outlined above. To do so would fill an entire book. There are many such lessons available for adoption, and these can often be adapted to manifest the principles we are stressing. But we shall include one lesson format that is highly adaptable to a range of problem issues.

The narrative technique of externalizing the problem is admirably suited to discussions of sensitive or controversial topics. It can, therefore, be used to powerful effect in a guidance lesson format adaptable to a variety of purposes. The key to this method is the use of the sociodramatic technique of "interviewing the problem" (Roth & Epston, 1996). For example, a lesson on racial prejudice, or on sexual harassment, or on bullying, or on homophobia can be built around a personification of the problem. Once personified, each of these problems can be engaged in a dramatization of the dominant discourse. With a little bit of practice, teachers and counselors can learn how to build a role-played conversation on one of these issues that is easy to instigate and fun to participate in, rather than heavily serious. The key is to locate the problem in social interactions, rather than in a person's nature. Here, then, is a plan for constructing a lesson based on this approach.

Introducing the Role Play

The first step is to introduce the topic and to tell the class that they are privileged to be present for a rare interview with, for example, "racial prejudice" today. In fact, racial prejudice has agreed, in a highly unusual departure from its usual practice of operating incognito, to give a press conference to a selected group of reporters. By sheer chance, this class has been designated as the group of reporters. Victims of racial prejudice everywhere will be eager to learn what racial prejudice has to say, so the "reporters" need to do a careful job of asking questions and listening to what racial prejudice has to say.

Be careful to say that it is not going to be an interview with a person who is prejudiced, but with racial prejudice itself. Everyone in the class is going to have a role to play, but the role does not involve any acting ability and the majority of students can play their role by staying in their seats. Point out that they are all going to have a chance to ask about many things that they might have wondered about racial prejudice. Explain that the aim of the exercise is to explore the relationship between the problem and people in their own school—that is, people like them. It is not about making anyone feel uncomfortable about their own attitudes. Instead, the focus will remain on understanding racial prejudice from the problem's perspective, rather than from the human perspective.

Role-Playing the Problem

Two or three volunteers need to be recruited to play the role of racial prejudice. Outgoing members of the class can be invited into this role. Students with a quick wit who have some status in the peer group are eminently suitable. The reason for having two or three volunteers is so that they can help each other, although the exercise can be done with one person playing the problem. Another reason for having several individuals play the problem is that they can each focus on different aspects of the problem. For example, while role-playing racial prejudice, each can be racial prejudice against a different ethnic group that is present in the school and can answer questions from that perspective. The complexities and subtleties of how racial prejudice operates can thus be dramatized. The role of racial prejudice can be concretized by telling a brief story, perhaps one that has recently happened in the school, in which racial prejudice had its way with people and wreaked its particular kind of havoc. This scenario should, of course, be as relevant as possible to the lives of the students, not an example of racial prejudice acting through adults with whom they will not identify.

Those role-playing the problem need to be given specific and clear instructions that they are not to think or speak as people at all. They are actually to be racial prejudice itself. They are the personification of a problem attitude that sometimes inserts itself into people's thoughts or behavior. They should be given a few minutes to prepare themselves to be racial prejudice by thinking about their particular aspect to emphasize and about some things they might want to get across in the subsequent interview. If necessary, the facilitator can help them get into their role by asking them a few questions in their role. Their subtly different roles may be stimulated by asking each volunteer to think of a situation from his or her experience in which racial prejudice has had an influence in someone's life. These scenarios can be prepared in advance and placed on a card for them to read, but it is better if they come from the students themselves.

Role-Playing News Reporters

The rest of the class is now invited to take on the role of news reporters who are gathered for a press conference granted by racial prejudice. You can assign them the names of TV networks, local TV stations, radio stations, magazines such as *Newsweek,* or newspapers. Instruct them that their task is to think up questions to ask racial prejudice. They can take a few minutes to prepare these questions. Explain that the kind of questions they should ask will enable everyone to learn about people's problems from racial prejudice's perspective. Remind them that it is rare for racial prejudice to grant such a news conference, and they should make the most of the opportunity. Their task will be to write an exposé of the tactics of racial prejudice so that their readers and viewers can be on the alert for its methods. See Box 10.1 for sample questions.

BOX 10.1
SAMPLE INTERVIEW QUESTIONS

Stage 1: Problem Exploration Questions

What are your purposes in life?

What are your intentions for this school?

What are your hopes and dreams for young people's future lives?

What gives you the most satisfaction?

What do you like to hear young people saying or doing?

What techniques do you use to get young people on your side?

How do you know when you are most effective?

(Continued)

(Continued)

What tricks or methods of persuasion do you use to get your own way?

Who is it easiest to work with?

What other problems are you friends with?

What makes your work easier?

What are some of your favorite methods of getting into someone's life?

What do you promise young people when they are a bit reluctant to listen?

What are some of the effects in a school that you especially aim to create?

What do you promise to give students, if they do your wishes?

What do you try to convince a person of, in order to persuade him or her?

Do you have different tactics with girls as opposed to boys? With people of different ethnicities?

Stage 2: Questions to Bring Out the Counter Story

What makes your work harder?

What would you count as failure?

What were your spectacular failures?

What do you lie awake at night and worry young people will do?

What makes you the most disappointed?

What actions by students most annoy you or make you nervous?

What social movements have you most disliked and why?

What ideas do you try and steer people away from?

What can students do that would make you give up and look elsewhere for people to win over?

What can students say back to you that undermines your efforts?

Are there any programs that make people immune to your influence?

What or who would you say are your most dangerous enemies?

What do you particularly dislike to hear students saying?

The Interview

With all the explanations given, it is now time to conduct the interview. The facilitator can start things off, if the reporters are slow to begin, by asking two or three example questions. This models the style of questions and shows how they are addressed to racial prejudice, rather than to a person.

There are two stages to the questioning, reflecting the practice of double listening. In the first stage, questions should be about exploring the problem; detailing its methods and tactics; and then mapping its effects, particularly its effects on people in the school. In the second stage, questions should be about the counter story—that is, about ways in which the problem fails to achieve its goals or becomes demoralized. Indications of possible failure can be accessed by asking what racial prejudice is worried about. Such failures should not be ascribed to chance or to the actions of the problem, but to the ways in which students take advantage of gaps in the power of the problem, or indeed, actively resist its influence. You can invite reporters to think of themselves as investigative journalists and encourage them to ask the really penetrating questions that will make racial prejudice squirm with discomfort. Elements of the counter story are accessed by asking racial prejudice tough questions that require it to "admit" its failures and weaknesses, confess its embarrassments, and acknowledge what it hates to see people doing to nullify its influence. Usually students can catch on to the problem exploration questions but need a little more help to master the second phase of questioning. The facilitator can scaffold these questions by modeling a few examples and by soliciting from the "reporters," for example, questions about what racial prejudice hates to see. The questions in Box 10.1 are not intended to be asked one after the other in a linear fashion. They are examples of possible questions, and students can be invited to formulate their own.

It is important for the facilitator to be alert for questions that create confusion by asking the role players to answer something that a problem could not really answer because it is something that only a person could speak about. Confusion can also be introduced by the role players of the problem if they inadvertently start speaking as a person influenced by racial prejudice, rather than as racial prejudice itself. If either of these things happens, the facilitator needs to quickly intervene and restore the roles and functions on which the conversation depends. This can be achieved by saying to racial prejudice something like, "Actually, that is a question that only a person could answer. You would probably have to just say, 'I don't know.'" The facilitator can also help scaffold the externalizing language by offering a rephrasing of either the question or the answer.

The interview can vary in length, depending on the time available, the creativity of the students, and the attention span of the class. It might take between 10 and 25 minutes. The reporters should take careful notes about what racial prejudice says and take particular care to capture the language of the problem. This language will contain references to the local nuances of the discourse of racial prejudice and of its counter story. It is wise to listen carefully so that follow-up discussions can use the exact resonant phrases from this discourse.

When the second part of the interview is completed, all students need to become themselves again. At least, those playing the problem need to separate from the role they have been playing. To help them de-role properly, the facilitator might ask them to stand and move seats and, as they move, to leave racial prejudice on the chair on which they have been sitting. When they have moved, ask them to say out loud to the class three ways in which they are different from the role they have been playing. Those who have been playing the role of investigative reporters need not be de-roled, since we would want students to continue to investigate how racial prejudice works and to identify its failures and worries.

After the Interview

Students typically have fun with this exercise, once they have warmed up to the task. The purpose is serious, but the approach to it is lighthearted and ironical. It therefore allows for serious topics to be addressed without generating uncomfortable heaviness in the conversation. Blame is forestalled before it can get started, and no one is put in the position of being shamed. At the same time, significant representations of the work done by the dominant discourse are enacted. It is, therefore, now slightly harder for these discourses to do their work behind people's backs in the future.

The worth of the exercise, however, does not just lie in the enactment of the interview. The effectiveness of it as a learning tool can be increased by the ways in which it is processed and extended. In this sense, the role-play drama can serve as an engaging prelude to a further discussion about the problem issue. Box 10.2 contains some sample discussion topics.

BOX 10.2
DISCUSSION TOPICS TO FOLLOW THE INTERVIEW

1. How honest do you think racial prejudice was?

2. Were there topics you would have liked to bring up that you could not think of how to phrase a question about?

3. What were the most important things that racial prejudice revealed?

4. What do you think it left out, glossed over, or failed to admit?

5. How big a problem do you think it is in our school? In our community?

6. Are there stories you can share of the work that racial prejudice does in our school? (Be careful to ensure that externalizing language continues to be used in discussing these stories.)

7. Who do you admire for setting an example of how to deal with this problem?

8. What further readings might we do to understand how racial prejudice works?

9. What would leaders such as Martin Luther King Jr. or Nelson Mandela advise about how to counter this problem?

10. How could the presence of this problem in our school be researched?

Dramatizing the Interview Material

A further step in developing the material produced through the interview with the problem can take place through the use of drama. One high school counselor (see Winslade & Monk, 2007) collaborated with the school drama teacher to generate a dramatic presentation about the issue of "racial taunts" that had arisen in his school. A drama class developed some enactments of typical instances that illustrated this problem and its effects on people, each derived from an interview with the problem. The result was a humorous but poignant drama in which the ideas about combating the influence of racism emerged completely from indigenous knowledge within the school. They then performed the drama in front of school assemblies. The school counselor followed up by visiting classes and talking to them about furthering the counterplot to the story of racism.

ACCEPT OR RESIST

We want to add one further example of a flexible lesson format to this chapter that makes use of sociodramatic methods to address conflict issues. It is specifically designed for constructing lessons aimed at dealing with the encounter with oppressive practices and can be applied to a variety of issues. In particular, this exercise invites students to reflect on scenarios in which they might find themselves faced with an oppressive practice and to consider how they might respond—that is, whether they might accept it or resist it in some way. The assumption of the exercise is that tactical decisions about choices of response are needed in the real world. It is also an assumption of the exercise that considered responses are likely to be more helpful than reactive responses. This work is adapted from an exercise developed by Augusto Boal (1992).

Developing the Scenario

The first step is to develop a scenario that will serve as the basis for the enactments to follow. This can be achieved in various ways. The facilitator can provide some brief stories, or the stories can be elicited from the class. The "interviewing the problem" exercise outlined above is an ideal way to do the latter. The former approach requires some extra steps to ensure that the scenario(s) provided are relevant to the life experience of students. Another alternative is to use movie clips of oppressive practices (for example, from the movie *Crash* or *Precious*) and then hold a conversation with the class about the relationship between what they have seen in the movie and what happens in their world. The aim is to develop a local scenario, rather than one from the movie. At the same time, care should be taken that the scenario is a generic one and that the class does not use the exercise to scapegoat any individual who is either present in the room or not present. The exercise works best when some detail is developed in the scenario, the characters are developed a little so that we know something of their background, and a timeline of events from the back-story is built up. Here are some questions designed to generate the scenario.

Can you say what the oppressive practice was in this story? (Remember to name the practice rather than naming the person as an oppressive person.)

Does that sort of thing happen here? Tell me some stories of what has happened in your experience. What is one story we can settle on to enact in this exercise?

What led up to the main event in this story? What was the background?

Who was the victim of an oppressive practice? What kind of person was he? What are his interests and his living situation? What does he value in life? Give him a name.

To whom does it matter what happened to the victim? Who cares about her? What would her perspective be? Give her a name.

What voices support the oppression? Who are some characters to represent this position? Give them some names.

What advice might each of these supporters of the victim or of the oppressive practices give to the victim?

Once the scenario that contains an oppressive practice has been developed, it can be built into a dramatic scenario. Class members can then be invited to play the role of each of the characters. Explain that the scenario will be enacted three times, and each time the focus will be on the response to the oppressive practice. There will be a different kind of response for each enactment. Each enactment is followed up by a discussion with the whole class, designed to invite them to think about the consequences of this kind of response.

Enactment 1

In the first enactment, the scene is played out with the protagonist instructed to make a decision to *accept* (rather than resist) the oppressive practice. The scene is played out just long enough for everyone to show some response to the protagonist's choice. It is followed up with a discussion about this choice. It should be recognized as a possible and sometimes realistic choice that people might make on occasion for sound reasons. The exercise is not about pathologizing the acceptance of oppression. The intention is rather to develop compassion among class members for how oppressive practices put people in positions where they often accept things that they would prefer not to. Here are some questions to guide the discussion that follows the enactment.

1. How did everyone react to the protagonist's acceptance of the oppression? What effect did it have on each person in the scene (including on the protagonist)?

2. (*To the whole class*) Why might a person choose to make this response? Which voices would support this? Which would oppose it?

3. What values might this choice express? What can you admire or not admire about the choice that expresses these values?

4. What might be the consequences and the risks of this choice?

Enactment 2

In the second enactment, the scene is played out again, but this time the protagonist chooses to resist the oppressive practice in some way. It is up to the protagonist to decide what form this resistance might take. If the protagonist cannot think of some form of resistance, the rest of the class can be consulted to brainstorm a list of ideas. From these ideas, the protagonist is invited to decide which one to choose. Once again, the scene is played out just long enough for everyone to show some response to the protagonist's choice. Once again, the whole class is then engaged in a discussion about the difference between acceptance and resistance to an oppressive practice. Here is a list of similar questions to guide the discussion.

1. How did everyone react to the protagonist's resistance of the oppression? What effect did it have on each person in the scene (including the protagonist)?

2. (*To the whole class*) Why might a person choose to make this response? Which voices would support this? Which would oppose it?

3. What values might this choice express? What can you admire or not admire about the choice of response?

4. What might be the consequences and the risks of this choice?

Enactment 3

In the third enactment, the same scene is played out for a third time. This time, the protagonist decides on a different method of resistance. The person playing the protagonist is asked to think about what happened in the previous enactment and to experiment with any variations, subtle or not so subtle, in how to respond. For variation, another member of the audience can be invited to play the role of the protagonist. The facilitator can ask, "Who has a different idea about how to resist an oppressive practice like this?" and then invite one person to demonstrate his or her idea by entering the scene and acting it out.

The aim of this third enactment is to open up consideration of the most effective forms of resistance, or of those that are more consistent with the preferred values of the class members. An implicit message (which can be made explicit) is that there are always choices in how we respond to oppressive practices. This is an expression of the narrative belief that life is multi-storied and of the poststructuralist idea that there is always a possible response to any oppressive practice. However, as Michel Foucault (2000) points out, sometimes expressions of resistance can be "muddled" (p. 155) rather than considered and, therefore, less effective in producing change. The invitation in this exercise is to think about how to respond to oppressive practices in ways that better express people's preferred values. Once again, though, discussion can be guided by the same list of questions as for the second enactment. Depending on the time available, the third enactment can be repeated for a fourth, fifth, or sixth time, or as many times as necessary.

In the final debrief, after all the enactments have been discussed, the facilitator should ask everyone in the class what they have learned from the whole exercise. Each of the role players should be thanked and carefully invited to leave their role behind. Attention should also be given to those who have played the role of the protagonists. What was it like for these people to be subjected to oppressive practices? And what was it like for them to choose from among several forms of response to these practices? Finally, everyone in the class should be invited to think about occasions when they have been in the role of dishing out oppressive practices.

SUMMARY

We have outlined in this chapter just two lesson formats. They are included here because they are adaptable to a variety of contexts and problem issues. There is, however, a range of other lessons that can be used to address issues that produce conflict in school communities. Facilitators may often need to be creative in the design of lessons that address local manifestations of problems.

What we have also tried to specify in this chapter are some principles for guiding the process of running such lessons. One of these is a preference for a non-blaming and non-pathologizing approach. This approach has several advantages. For one thing, it locates problems where they belong—in the repetition of harmful discourses, rather than making problem issues isomorphic with what lies in the hearts of individuals. For another, this approach produces a more fruitful conversation that avoids getting bogged down in accusation and defensiveness. For another thing, this approach allows for the statement of counter stories to exist alongside dominant discourses of oppression. They are optimistic lessons in their use of humor, irony, and lightness in the cause of opposing oppression. As a result, they have the potential to connect with the subtleties of local problems. Finally, in each of these lessons, the knowledge that is foregrounded is the local knowledge of the participants, rather than the formal knowledge of adults or of the academic world. These lessons exhibit a profound trust in the best selves that young people can bring to the discussion. They are not naïve in assuming that young people always act out of these best selves. But in order for their best selves to grow stronger, they must be given a chance to be expressed.

QUESTIONS FOR REFLECTION

1. What are the patterns of oppressive practice you can identify as present in the discourse of your school?

2. How are those oppressive practices manifested in the local expressions of discourse in the school community?

3. How can a school counselor listen to the discourses at work in a school community?

4. What lessons about the choice to accept or resist would you want students to learn?

QUESTIONS FOR RESEARCH

1. What might a discourse analysis of teacher and student talk in a school reveal about local expressions of oppression?

2. How might student learnings from an "interviewing the problem" exercise be evaluated?

3. What differences might the use of such guidance lessons effect in a school's climate?

4. What might a close study of the meanings generated in one guidance lesson yield in terms of how the process works?

11

"Facing Up to Violence" Groups

THE VALUE OF GROUP COUNSELING FOR CHANGING VIOLENT BEHAVIOR

Group counseling is an economical way of providing a service for a number of young people at the same time. It economizes on counselor time, and it also makes it possible for young people to learn from each other, rather than from direct individual experience. Adolescents, especially, are known to be influenced by the views of their peers, and group counseling makes use of the relational influences that young people can have on each other. It makes sense, therefore, to use groups in schools to facilitate violence reduction.

Group counseling recognizes too that problem behaviors, including violent and abusive ones, are often habitual and patterned. They are sometimes not just an outgrowth of one conflict between individuals, but are also the effect of assumptions that have been internalized over time and have formed into a nexus of attitudes, beliefs, and repeated performances. A group can be dedicated to changing the pattern of these performances so that the incidence of violence in a school community is reduced.

Consider for a moment the use of the word *performances* in the last sentence. It is a deliberate choice over the more common word, *behaviors*. Stressing the performative quality of young persons' expressions of aggression brings into view more of the relational dimension. It gestures toward the likelihood that an action has an audience in mind on whom the actor desires an effect. It suggests that we ask questions about intended relational effects, rather than about antecedent causes.

By contrast, the usual use of the word *behavior* assumes the individual is at the center of his or her own universe. We are more likely to ask questions about the internal motivation of the person than about the intended effect on others. The difference is about a more relational psychology than an essentialist one. From an individualistic perspective, behaviors emerge from within more than they are directed at others. They are conditioned more than they are intentional.

The preference for a relational psychology leads us to pay attention to power relations in human performances. Very often (although we hesitate to say always), people use violence to have an effect on others, rather than to express something that lies within them. Michel Foucault (1982) gave us a compelling definition of power. He described it as any "action upon the actions of others" (p. 220). By no means are all "actions upon the actions of others" problematic or violent. Some exercising of power relations is quite normal and commonplace. The problems arise when such actions cross ethical boundaries and enter the territory of coercion and domination.

Group counseling that seeks to make a difference in the experiences of violence by young people in a school should start from this assumption—that a student who performs an act of violence is engaged in an act of power. Such an action sets in motion a relational consequence, which, in the end, obliges him or her to be responsible for the harm done. Providing opportunities for young people to learn this lesson is the object of many of the processes described in this book.

Group counseling that helps young people face up to violence tries to interrupt the rapidly firing pathways of assumption that violence is natural and justified. Slowing these pathways of assumption down and opening them up to scrutiny allow students to think about violence in ways they have possibly never done before. Once they are engaged in this kind of reflection, it becomes harder to respond in the same habitual ways in future. In the vacuum thus created, new habits, or new stories, can start to form. Of course, it is easy to say these things in theory. The practice, however, is more demanding.

WHY NOT ANGER MANAGEMENT?

You may have noticed we did not call this chapter "Anger Management Groups." Group counseling with this title has become very common, to the extent that we have sometimes used this name for groups on the grounds of its recognizability. But it is not our preference. The problem is that the concept of "anger management" assumes something about the origin of violent actions. Behind this assumption is the old 19th-century psychological metaphor of the steam engine in which anger exists in a pressure chamber. As long as the lid is kept on it and it is controlled properly, it will not risk "boiling over" and escaping into the person "losing it."

On the assumption that aggression is about the release of emotion from within, violence is explained first by the mechanism of emotional release from within the pressure chamber and, second, by the use of the repression assumption. The more that emotion is held down and repressed, the more rapidly and uncontrollably it will be released. This hydraulic theory of anger management as emotional expression from within the individual leads anger management groups to teach effective means of emotional release, rather than allowing anger to build up until it blows out uncontrollably.

There has, of course, been some updating of the 19th-century steam engine metaphor. It has been replaced in many places by the 20th-century metaphors of computer systems. In this vein, angry responses are "programmed" into people and need to be "reprogrammed." The anger module needs to be replaced with new software that responds in a different way.

The assumption that acts of violence and aggression are always about controlling the emotion of anger is, however, a dubious one. It does not take into account aggression that is cool and calculated. Many people do violent things without feeling anger rise up within them at all. Indeed, the approaches we have referred to above focus very heavily on the internal psychology of the person who commits a violent act, as if this person does not live in a social context.

What we are proposing here is an approach to antiviolence group work that is built on more relational assumptions. We work on the assumption that violence is more often about the desire for power and control over others than about release of emotion. Even when this is not a consciously formed desire, it may be an effect that can be exploited. For example, think of the person who develops a temper tantrum habit. This person may find that the habit produces effects in others that mean that the person will be responded to more than if she did not throw the tantrum. Sometimes, however, there is little anger involved, or perhaps anger may best be thought of as a by-product of violence rather than as the source of it. A group based on these assumptions will not seek to create blame and shame about violence, so much as to explore group members' preferences for violence-free lifestyles and to grow identity stories and relational performances that fit with these preferences.

GENDER AND FACING UP TO VIOLENCE

In our experience, it is best for facing up to violence groups to be gender-specific. It is not impossible in some circumstances for mixed gender groups to happen, but in many contexts, the gender discourses at play make the task of creating the right kind of reflective environment very hard to achieve.

For a start, male violence is far more common than female violence. To be sure, it is now more common for young women to use violence than it used to be. But incitements to violence as a facet of identity development are still far more persuasively directed at young men. You only have to think of the action movies and video games with male heroes in them, and this becomes obvious.

Male and female violence is also typically different in character, even though there may be points of overlap. Female violence is not always about the use of excessive force, as we discussed in Chapter 1. Often, girls use relational aggression against other girls to very painful effect, but boys are not so subtle.

The cultural context of male violence against women also needs to be taken into account in school violence. It is in schools, as well as in family contexts, that both males and females learn the patterns of response that will later become manifest in the violence that occurs in families. Although there are many debates about the incidence of domestic violence, it is generally accepted that the rate of such violence perpetrated by males against females is considerably higher than the reverse (Mirlees-Black & Byron, 1996; Tjaden & Thoennes, 2000). While women can also be violent and should not be excused for such actions, the overwhelming majority of domestic violence is committed by men against women, and women are more likely than men to be frightened, to be seriously injured, and to seek medical help (Mirlees-Black & Byron, 1996). What's more, this fact is implicitly understood by both boys and girls in schools, even without being spoken about directly. Such is the power of dominant discourse.

One of the most powerful rationales for challenging male domestic violence is the argument that family violence needs to be understood as an expression of the desire for "power and control," rather than as an expression of anger within. This is the assumption behind many feminist analyses of family violence and also has been made widely popular in social work circles by the Duluth program (Pence & Paymar, 1993). A number of successful intervention programs have been built on these foundational assumptions. The power and control model does not necessarily account for all forms of violence, however. Particularly, it does not account for violence done in self-defense, for example, nor does it account for female violence in the way that it does for male violence. The reasons for this are that the use of violence to intimidate and control does not happen in a social vacuum. It needs to be supported by a general discourse that makes male authority and female submissiveness the norm. Despite the work done by feminists to undermine this discourse, it still has currency in the minds of many men and women.

Among young people in schools, this discourse has not yet reached its full expression. It is, however, present in nascent form. In mixed-gender counseling groups, it can become manifest as dominating performance in conversation by male students, particularly when the boys outnumber the girls, which forces the girls to defer. It will be subtly expressed in jokes and laughter, designed to come across as playful courtship displays. As such, it is hard to criticize in itself, but, in its effects, it can interfere with a group establishing the kinds of reflective and trusting climate that enables productive counseling work to take place. Same-gender groups avoid the interference.

In our experience, too, productive work to deconstruct the gendered aspects of violence are easier to achieve in same-gender groups. Girls find it easier to speak up about what they know implicitly about the effects of male patterns of controlling behavior, and boys are more likely to acknowledge their own implicit discomfort with such behavior in a context where they do not have to lose face in front of girls in order to do so.

PRINCIPLES OF "FACING UP TO VIOLENCE" GROUP COUNSELING

There are five main principles for facing up to violence group work in schools. The first principle is to avoid supporting essentializing explanations for violence. An essentializing explanation is one that makes violence seem natural. "This is just how it is," people will say in justification for violating others. "It is just human nature," another will remark. "It is part of my culture to be physically strong," is a variation that relies on an essentialist conception of culture. "Fighting is part of life, especially around my neighborhood." Group members will very likely expect the group leaders to take up a strongly antiviolence stance, and they are ready for a battle of wits, with these essentializing stock expressions at their fingertips.

As a group leader, it is important to be very up front about your own preference for nonviolent solutions to life situations without implicitly putting down the life experiences of the group members. They are usually right in that this is what they have known. The secret is to make this knowledge *contingent,* rather than essential. If it is an expression of a contingent choice, then there are implicitly other choices that can be made.

The second principle is to avoid getting into a struggle in which the group leader is arguing for a violence-free lifestyle and trying to convince group members to agree. When this happens, group members will resist and talk themselves more into a position of justifying violence. The alternative stance does not require the group leader to be neutral or to take up a provocative position of advocating for violence. Instead, the leader asks a series of questions that offer the group members the chance to argue against violence. This can be done in an abstract way at first, rather than personalizing. For example, ask group members, "What would you say are the problems with an atmosphere of bullying in a school?" A useful follow-up question might be, "Why do you think that is a problem?"

The third principle is to accept and be curious about whatever group members say at this point, and to avoid pointing out to group members their "hypocrisy" when their espoused theories do not match their theories-in-use (Argyris & Schön, 1974). To do so will close down the conversation and limit the build-up of trust in the group. It is better to accept discrepancies between preferred perspectives and actual behavior, especially at first. The chance for members to choose between lifestyles will come later.

The fourth principle is to avoid conversations that end up justifying violent behavior. For example, avoid asking people *why* they did a violent act. The question why will usually produce a justification and a rationalization for the violence. As group members give voice to these justifications, they strengthen them. On the social constructionist principle that what we speak about, we materialize, it makes more sense to talk more about nonviolent preferences.

What might a group leader do when group members still speak about violence in terms that emphasize how justified it is? To oppose such expressions is not likely to work. It will only provoke resistance and further intensification of these expressions. The secret at this point is again to render such justifications as possibilities that are contingent, rather than essential. The narrative practice of externalizing conversation is very useful here. Group leaders can seek to externalize either the behavior itself or, better, the justifications or reasons for violence, and then invite group members into conversations about how they or others get persuaded by these justifications.

The fifth principle to emphasize is based on the book *Invitations to Responsibility* by Alan Jenkins (1990). This eminently practical book outlines an effective approach to engaging men who have been violent and abusive in their families in therapeutic conversations that bring about change. Jenkins draws explicitly on narrative principles to engage with people who have committed violent acts. He works from the assumption that even those who commit awful violent acts would prefer to have peaceful and respectful relationships with others. They have also, however, internalized from the discourse around them assumptions that *restrain* them from being the more peaceful, respectful person that they would rather be. Violence is only possible because preferences for more peaceful relationships are sufficiently restrained by internalized cultural forces. The aim of group counseling, therefore, is to remove the restraints and to allow more peaceful stories to flower. This requires a group climate in which members separate from the assumptions that restrain peaceable identity narratives and identify more closely with the respectful person that they would rather be.

We can summarize these principles in a set of statements as follows.

BOX 11.1
PRINCIPLES FOR GROUP COUNSELING

- Decline to accept justifications for violence that make it seem natural and essential.
- Avoid direct confrontation of group members. Instead, invite group members to confront the problem.
- Accept (at first) discrepancies between words and actions, and invite group members to expand on their words of opposition to violence.
- Avoid asking "why" questions that elicit justifications for violence.
- Identify and externalize the restraints on taking responsibility, and invite the group members to challenge these.
- Acknowledge and highlight any evidence of accepting responsibility.

A PLAN FOR A "FACING UP TO VIOLENCE" GROUP

Having addressed the operating principles, we shall now outline a practical plan for running a group. It will include a range of sample questions that can be used to initiate lines of inquiry in a group. These are not intended to be prescriptive questions so much as suggested questions that can be used.

Target Group

This group is intended for those who have been in trouble at school or in the community for expressions of anger or violence problems. They may have been suspended or referred by the courts, or they may be identified by teachers or counselors on the basis of aggressive or violent actions at school.

Objectives

- Group members will have the chance to reflect upon the place that anger or violence has in their lives at school and the life that it has planned out for them.
- They will explore options for establishing directions of their own that anger or violence does not dictate for them.
- They will be given the opportunity to make commitments to a violence-free lifestyle and to develop skills and strategies to support that commitment.

Purpose of the Group

How a group succeeds depends on a clear statement of intention at the start. Here is a list of points to stress at the start of a group, before introductions have been made.

- "This group has been referred by the school counselors and administrators because they are concerned about issues of violence.
- "We don't think it helps to just punish people for problems with violence. The idea of this group is to give you a chance to think about and to have your say about the influence of violence in your life. It is a chance to make a difference for yourself.
- "We are not interested in making you into a perfect student. In fact, we will not make you into anything. That will be your choice.
- "We will also not make you feel bad or ashamed or blame you for anything from the past. Our aim is to treat you as intelligent people who can think and have a say in your own lives and not just let violence have its own way.
- "The group is based on the assumption that everyone can control anger and adopt violence-free lifestyles and on a clear preference for these. It is aimed to help you consider this as a goal for yourselves, but will not force you to adopt any particular view.
- "This group will last for eight [or however many] sessions and will take place in this room once a week on these days: _____."

Ground Rules

As with any group, ground rules should be negotiated and developed with the group members. However, there are several points that need to be carefully attended to, given the focus of the group.

The first concern is that confidentiality is limited to situations in which there is no threat of harm to the students or to someone else. Sometimes you will want to check with a victim whom a group member has harmed to ensure that this person has not been threatened again. Such checking is not a breach of confidentiality so much as an expression of ethical practice. It is also important that no violence be tolerated in the group itself. Group leaders should underline their ethical, and sometimes legal, responsibility to report any situation outside the group where harm is possible and imminent.

Establish Reasons for Referral

Referral to such a group is often mandated rather than completely voluntary. This need not be a hindrance to the success of the group. Research shows that mandated group members still get personal value from group counseling (Corey, Corey, & Corey, 2010), even when they at first express reluctance to attend. It is, nevertheless, wise to acknowledge that some or all group members are present under duress and to be curious about what each person thinks about that. Even for a group member to acknowledge that he or she does not want to be there and is only there because he has to be is an honest statement that deserves to be appreciated:

"Thank you for being up front about that—and for coming along, despite the fact that it wasn't your first choice. I still hope that you will get something of value for yourself out of the group, since you have to be here."

At the same time, we would not take at complete face value statements of reluctance to be present. A person's motivation to attend a group is seldom completely positive or negative. In most cases, there are competing stories clamoring for attention within us. Those who are attending voluntarily may have stories of suspicion about the group that may urge them to pull out. And those who are mandated to attend may harbor hope of gaining from the group, even though they lose less face to say they are not attending voluntarily. It is, therefore, useful to ask questions that acknowledge these competing internal stories, rather than to force people into one or the other camp.

For example, a group leader can ask the following:

"How much is attendance here voluntary for you?"

"Who said you should be here? What did you think of that?"

"How much do you resent being told to be here and how much are you okay about being here? Can you put a percentage on that, for example, 50/50?"

"Are you willing to get something for yourselves from the group?"

Affirm Group Members' Courage in Being Present

Early in the group, it is useful to acknowledge the courage it takes to face up to violence. Doing so helps build trust in the group and in the leadership. This acknowledgment can be given in the form of a simple statement, or it can underlie some questions that are asked for group members to respond to. Here is an example of a statement of acknowledgment:

> It takes a lot of courage to face up to issues of anger and violence. It is much easier to not do so. A lot of people don't even have the courage to come, even when they are told to. Sometimes people deeply regret things that they have done and feel so ashamed that they can't even face up to admitting to themselves that they did that—let alone admitting it to other people. We also want to acknowledge that people who get into difficulty with anger and violence have sometimes been victims of other people's violence too. So that makes it doubly courageous to attend a group like this. So thank you for coming. We have a few questions to ask about that. We want to apologize for having to ask questions to make this group work, and we want you to tell us if we ask too many.

Here are some examples of questions that acknowledge group members' choice to be part of the group. Alan Jenkins (1990) calls these questions "irresistible invitations" to responsibility. They are designed to draw upon the discourses of strength and physical courage that are often more closely associated with perpetrating violence than with facing up to violence. They are, therefore, deconstructive questions in the sense that they call on one discourse to be put to a different use than it normally is.

> "Can you handle us asking questions about your experiences of violence, or is that too much for you?"

> "Does it take more strength to talk about these issues or more strength to not talk about them? Why?"

> "What do you think it says about you that you came here today?"

> "Is it in any way an exaggeration to think that the first success we have had is that we are all here? How did you succeed in coming through the door, rather than skipping this meeting?"

Invite the Group Members to Argue for a Violence-Free Lifestyle

The next part of the group is designed to get the group talking about anger and violence in general terms, rather than in terms of their own experience. These questions are designed to stimulate general discussion in the abstract. Rather than setting up the group leader as the expert on what is wrong with violence, these questions call forth the group members' knowledge of the problems violence and aggression can cause.

Asking these kinds of questions helps the group leader to avoid arguing for these things and trying to persuade group members to join him. It is more effective to let the arguments come from the group. If they equivocate, make the questions more stark. For example, if group members start to engage in arguments that justify violence, you can respond with something like this:

"So do you think what those guys did at Columbine High School was okay? Why not?"

Here are some sample questions along these lines:

"In your view, is it better to get people to do what you want by threat and violence or by their choice?"

"When other people are trying to get you to do what they want, which do you prefer?"

"Some men think it is okay to bash their wives and to beat up little kids. What do you think is wrong with that?"

"What is wrong with people bringing knives and guns to school and using them to intimidate others?"

"Would you prefer relationships with others at school, with your girlfriend, or with family members (or wherever the problem of violence has been expressed) that are full of violence and fear or full of respect and free of violence?"

"What would you call it when violence and aggression are not present in a relationship?"

"Why is it better? What are the advantages of this type of relationship?"

"Some people say that people deserve to be beaten. Do you agree? Why or why not?"

In the course of this discussion, some people may make strong rational commitments against violence and suggest that they will never again do the things that previously got them into trouble. In this case, ask them to argue for this position more strongly. For example, the group leader can ask the following:

"So do you feel strongly about that? How strongly do you feel?"

"How did you reach that decision?"

"What sorts of reasons do you have for that position?"

"Are you confident that you can hold onto that position if you are provoked?"

These questions are not intended to be asked in a sarcastic way or in any way to show people up to be hypocritical. They only work if they are asked out of genuine curiosity and interest in what the person might say. At the end of this section of the group, it is useful to thank group members for their arguments against violence and aggression, "because they give us a lot to work with."

Share Why They Are Here

Having invited group members to argue against violence, we are now ready to confront the reasons they were referred to the group. These reasons can now be positioned as contradictions to their expressed values in favor of nonviolent and peaceful behavior. Group leaders should not play a game of "Gotcha!" here. The narrative perspective is that people are multi-storied. There will always be places where our actions do not gel with our values. What is important is to frame the violent actions as an aberration from their expressed values, rather than as an expression of who they are.

The next conversation is, therefore, best done as a round in which each person is asked to speak in a matter-of-fact way. Here is a suggested way to introduce the round.

> We appreciate the values you have just expressed, but we all know that you are here because, on at least one occasion, your preferences for a violence-free lifestyle have not won out and you have been involved in aggression or violence. If you are strong enough to be able to handle this, can we ask you now to tell us briefly the story of what happened. If you are not feeling strong enough to handle it right now, you can just say "pass."

As group members tell their story, group leaders should simply accept each story and thank them for being honest. Do not get drawn into a concern about hypocrisy, if there are discrepancies between their espoused nonviolence and their violent practice. You may need to ask questions, however, to elicit the stories. Make these what, when, where, and how questions. Avoid "why" questions at this point, because these can invite forward justificatory discourses. Here are examples of clarifying questions that can be asked.

"What was the first thing that happened?"

"What did you think when he/she said/did that? What did you say/do/want to do?"

"What do you think he/she was feeling?"

"What happened next?"

"Can you describe what exactly you did that was aggressive or violent? How did you do that exactly? How many times? How and where did you hit her?"

There may be some balking at being honest in this phase. They may also be some minimizing of the violence ("I only gave him a little tap"). Meet this with further affirmation of the courage it takes to face up to these things. Perhaps ask some further questions along these lines:

"Are you ready to talk about this?"

"A lot of people run away from talking about this. Are you able to do so?"

"Can you handle it? Are you strong enough to be honest?"

"I respect you for speaking so frankly. Is this the first time you have done that?"

This discussion should end with a summary of the contrast between the intentions and beliefs expressed in the group that violence and aggression are not good things and the preference for respectful relationships and, on the other hand, these experiences where their beliefs have been restrained, or set in the background, and aggression or violence has taken over.

Discuss How People Get Recruited Into Violent Behavior

The next step is to deconstruct the assumptions and beliefs that support the use of violence and restrain people from expressing their preferences for a more peaceful life. The aim here is to understand how people get recruited into violent behavior, despite their preferences for more respectful relationships. The phrase "get recruited" is important because it signals the role played by the cultural context, and by the discourses that circulate within it, in making violence seem natural and normal. It assumes an anti-essentialist account of how violence is engendered in people's lives.

Group leaders can be creative here about the topical influences in the media, in movies, and in songs, and invite group members to unpack the messages therein. Discussion should move from the general to the personal. As each message is unpacked, group members should be asked about its relevance in their own community and in their own experience. Here are some questions to guide this discussion. Each is a line of inquiry leading into a conversation, rather than a single question.

"It is not surprising that violence exists. We are bombarded with invitations to use violence to find solutions to problems every day, every time we turn on a TV or use a video game. What is more interesting is what specifically stops you all from carrying out intentions to not be aggressive or violent."

"What are the ideas and arguments that support violence?"

"How do those thoughts or ideas get so strong?"

"How much influence do they have over you? Is it total control, or do they have limits?"

"How do particular stories of what it means to be a man or a woman sometimes support violence?"

"What messages about race and ethnicity make it easier for people to get caught up in violence?"

"Is violence more likely to happen among people who are wealthy or people who are poor? Why is that?"

"What is it about the culture of gangs that often leads to violence?"

"How much do family influences support violence?"

"How have you been recruited into the pathway that violence lays out?"

Inquire Into the Effects of Violence

Now it is time to explore the effects of violence in people's lives. If the group is ready to do so, the effects of violence can be explored directly in relation to the stories already shared from group members' lives. On the other hand, the group leader may judge that group members are not yet comfortable facing up to the effects of their own actions. In this case, an intermediate step is to tell a story and discuss the effects of violence in this story.

Which effects should be discussed? The aim should be to seek out a breadth of effects. Counselors often tend to focus on emotional effects (fear, anger, shame), and these are important to document. It is, however, also important to examine other effects and to add them to the list. Relational effects are very important because emotional effects tend to concentrate attention on the individual in his isolated state. Violence tears at the fabric of relationship in very powerful ways. It establishes uneven and unjust power relations and interrupts loyalties, friendships, family connections, and personal commitments. Health effects should not be overlooked either. Violence causes damage to bodies and, even when medical attention is not required, in the aftermath of violent actions people often experience bruises and cuts, lose sleep, and suffer from bodily tensions (headaches, stomach tension, backaches). Then there are the costs of violence in monetary terms (for example, doctors' bills) and in terms of time spent worrying, obsessing, missing work, or abandoning other activities.

Breadth of exploration is also important in terms of the number of people affected by an act of violence. Group members should not just focus on themselves in noticing the effects of violence, nor should the ostensible victim be considered the only person affected. Effects on witnesses and bystanders should be taken into account, as should effects on family members who hear about an incident later. Developing a full list of those affected is often quite surprising for individuals who are myopic in their focus on their own responses. Empathy for others can mitigate against further violence, and this exploration helps develop it. It should, therefore, not be cut short, and it is important to ask repeatedly, "What else?" in order to elicit greater detail in storying the effects of violence, especially after the more obvious effects have been listed.

The word *listed* also suggests the value of using a whiteboard to accumulate a diagrammatic or visual representation of the effects of violence so that they are seen in graphic form. The circle diagrams featured in Chapter 6 can be used or a simple list constructed. It can be powerfully motivating toward change for people to see this list growing before their eyes as the full effects of even one violent action are studied.

Identify the Triggers That Set Off Temper

As a result of the cultural influences that support violence, individuals often develop patterns of response to triggers from other people that set off violent responses. Sometimes this can be experienced as losing one's temper, but not always. In order to interrupt these responses, it is often useful to identify the triggers that set a person off. This is achieved by taking an incident of violence and retracing it step by step, carefully identifying what happened, and then what happened next in the sequence of interactions. Often this means slowing down the narrative so that the various steps in the process can be separated. When this is done, a pattern of response can emerge into view that can then be externalized and reexamined.

Generate Identity Descriptions

The next discussion asks questions about the identity stories produced in people. Identities should not be treated as emerging from the inside out, so much as negotiated in social interactions. People develop reputations as a result of violent acts that may not fit with how they want to be known. They may be totalizations built on the basis of a narrow range of behaviors. The group leader should acknowledge the power of reputations and the effects of power relations on identity stories, while at the same time keeping these stories contingent and available for change. Here are questions that can be used as lines of inquiry in this discussion:

"In your experience at school, what sorts of words are used to describe kids whom aggression and violence visit fairly frequently?"

"Are these descriptions always true?"

"Are they positive or negative or something else?"

"Are they fair?"

"Are they helpful? If so, for whom are they the most helpful?"

"What sort of future do these identity stories have planned out for you?"

You can also invite students to draw pictures to label these identity descriptions. Make sure, though, that they do not label them as persons, but as externalized names.

Grow the Counter Story

Now it is time to invite group members to make choices and to state their preferences for a counter story to the story of aggression and violence. Hopefully, the work done already has built a scaffold, which makes it easy for group members to choose nonviolent and peaceful relations. But it still needs to be a choice. The group leader cannot make this choice for the group and then attempt to persuade the group members to join in. Instead, the group leader should summarize what the group members have said about the effects of violence and then invite them to take a stand in relation to these effects. Do they want these effects to continue to occur, or do they want to stand for a different way of relating? For example, the leader may say something like this:

"You have told me about the effects that violence has on you and on other people. Do you think this is just something that has to be and you just have to go along with it, or would you prefer something better?"

Other questions might be like this:

"Do you want other people to be afraid of your violence or not?"

"Is it okay to allow these effects to keep on happening, or would you prefer something different?"

"If you are opposed to violence and its effects, what are your personal preferences for your relationships?"

These questions are simple choices between two options. It is easy to step into one choice or the other with only a small commitment. As group members begin to make this small choice, they can be invited to take a larger leap into the articulation of their personal preferred story of nonviolence. Asking them why is a start. Or they can simply be asked to say more about their preference for nonviolence or for peaceful relations.

Once there is even a small movement toward a new story, the group leader needs now to concentrate on growing this story. The rest of this chapter will outline a range of possible avenues for development of this counter story. They can be taken in any order or they can be combined together in response to what group members say.

Inquire Into the Taking of New Action

One option is to ask whether group members are ready to make changes, to try something new, or to experiment a little. If they are, then the group can flesh out the details of exactly when and where and how these changes can be implemented. As a group member speaks to an intention to make a change, the group leader's task shifts to asking questions about what could go wrong (*What would you do if . . . ?*). Such questions invite group members to consider how to overcome predictable obstacles.

Identify the History of New Action

There is a strong chance that ideas about changes group members want to make may have a history in their experience. It pays, therefore, to ask for this history. It may be a subjugated history, but it is nevertheless potentially important. Here are some questions that can be asked in this line of inquiry:

"Have you noticed times in the past when you have stood up to aggression and violence?"

"Have you had an intention to do so?"

"Are there times when you were not sucked in?"

"Are there other people you have respected who knew how to avoid getting caught up by violence? What was their secret?"

Learn About Danger Signs

Developing the new story often involves learning about sequences of thought and action that lead people into potentially violent responses. There is always a lead up. Violence never erupts spontaneously. Once these patterns and sequences are identified, they can be interrupted before they get out of control. Group members can study through subsequent group meetings how these sequences work. Discussions of this kind can be held around the following questions:

"What are the things that lead up to aggression and violence taking control?"

"What are the likely triggers for you to get angry?"

"How do you know when you might go too far?"

"How might you avoid letting aggression or anger take control at these times?"

Share Stories of Success and Alternative Knowledges

The mere fact that group members are thinking about and reflecting upon these issues in the group will likely lead to small changes in their behavior. At each group meeting, time should be allocated for sharing stories of success. At first, however, the dominant story of violence and aggression will scarcely allow these successes to be noticed. When asked about them, group members will most likely demur. Persistence is needed in this inquiry so that the small successes can be brought out. When a unique outcome is identified, it needs to be storied a little in order to grow in significance. Details need to be explored. Questions that can help grow this significance include the following:

"How did you do that?"

"What did it take to do that? What sorts of thoughts or techniques?"

"How did you prepare yourself to act differently?"

"How do you know this occasion wasn't a fluke?"

"Who would be least surprised to know that you had done this?"

Ideas for combating violence can be dignified by being documented as the group develops. Maps can be made on poster paper of the group's knowledge in response to the questions below. A group document called something like "Secret Antiviolence Knowledge" can be drawn up. It will be shared knowledge, often hard-won through collective experience. Each group member could be given a copy. This knowledge can be given greater credence by being linked to the ideas of well-known community leaders or artists or sportspersons. Ideas about change can thus be strengthened through giving group members a sense that they are participating in something bigger than themselves. Here are some lines of inquiry for this conversation:

"When you need to defend against the influence of anger or aggression, what have you learned to think about?"

"What is it useful to remember in order to limit the influence of anger and aggression in your life?"

"What have you learned about how to support each other against the influence of anger or aggression?"

Develop Alternative Stories of Identity

As little shifts in practice emerge, one way to strengthen them is to link them to alternative identity stories that may have been hitherto masked or underdeveloped. There are likely to exist stories of calmness or peacefulness or respect somewhere in everyone's range of personal narratives. Group leaders can ask about these in response to the sharing of counter stories. Here are some questions designed to bring forward such alternative identities:

"What personal qualities do you have that are not noticed when you are dominated by anger and aggression?"

"How can you avoid the influence of anger or aggression but not be thought of as 'weak'?"

"What's a name we could give to this kind of identity?"

"How can you express your sense of injustice when you see it happening to others, without inviting anger and aggression onto yourself?"

Restoration

As we saw in the chapter on restorative practices (Chapter 7), a strong counter story can involve the commitment to setting right the harm that has previously been done by acts of aggression. Putting things right demonstrates a commitment to change. It is not always easy to do and may take substantial courage. And it may sometimes be rejected by the other person. It can at least be canvassed with the following lines of inquiry.

"How do you set things right again after you have hurt someone else?"

"Is an apology possible? Is it enough?"

"Are you strong enough to listen to the effects of your anger on the other person(s)?"

"How can you demonstrate your desire to set things right? How can you sustain this over time?"

Predict Relapse

Once counter stories have been developed to the point that group members have become enthusiastic about them, group leaders can help strengthen them further by predicting relapses when the initial novelty wears off. Doing so helps prepare group members for this possibility and makes it less devastating when it happens. Here are some examples of what might be said:

> "We respect the efforts you have made in this group to address aggression and violence. Since life is not perfect, however, and you are not in complete control of everything around you, it is possible that anger and violence might return and try and win you back. How might it do this? How might you prevent this from happening?"

> "Does anyone have any examples of this kind of thing happening to them?"

> "How will you sustain the changes you have made after the novelty wears off?"

Celebrations

It is important to celebrate the success that the group has produced. Certificates can be given out to recognize achievements. A ritual celebration event can be held in which the certificates are awarded, and each group member can invite one person to attend. Changes can also be publicized by asking teachers to notice differences. Group members can also be asked whether they are willing to be consulted to help other young people in the future who might have similar struggles. They can be asked to make a list of pieces of advice to offer such people.

SUMMARY

This chapter outlines a range of ideas for constructing a "facing up to violence" group. The rationale for this kind of group differs from common approaches to "anger management." It is not a recipe to be followed slavishly. It is intended to be a list of resources rather than a prescription, and things may not always run in exactly this sequence. The important thing is the spirit in which the group is run. This spirit should be based not on applying an expert fix to the students, but on seeking out and documenting their knowledge and their preferences all the way along.

QUESTIONS FOR REFLECTION

1. What are the assumptions about the causes of violence built into the activities in common anger management programs?

2. What stands out for you in the principles for the groups outlined in this chapter?

3. How can group leaders show respect for group members' experience without slipping into collusion with violent actions?

QUESTIONS FOR RESEARCH

1. What are the most common arguments students raise for why they cannot change violent behavior?

2. What are the gender differences in violent behavior and in the justifications for violence?

3. How can changes in response to others made by participants in "facing up to violence" groups be evaluated?

4. How can the effects of these changes on others be evaluated?

12

Putting It All Together

TYING THE THREADS TOGETHER

It remains to tie together again the threads that we have separated out into different strands through the preceding chapters. To do this, we reiterate here some of the principles on which this book is based. We also make some final comments on an overall conflict management strategy in a school. And we address the question of how to choose from among the conflict resolution strategies outlined in the book.

We have consistently argued for a way of resolving conflict and addressing violence that views conflict as a product of the relationships that make up our world. To some degree, conflict is a normal outcome of difference between people, and learning to live with difference is a major learning task of being at school. It is just as important as learning mathematical or literary skills, for example.

Our emphasis has been on articulating practices that are consistent with the idea that "The person is not the problem; the problem is the problem." Addressing conflict issues is the task of conflict resolution work, not assigning blame. There is a trade-off between face-saving and identifying a path forward founded on a commitment to peace and understanding. To walk this path requires commitment, and not everyone in a school community will choose to walk it—teachers as well as students. Nothing in this book is a panacea, and there are no guarantees for happy endings every time. But neither are any of the alternative approaches able to offer that. Punishment, for example, regularly backfires. Zero tolerance sounds attractive in what it promises but has been shown to fall far short of its promise.

These methods will, we hope, appeal to the better angels in a school community and will help people shift from a conflict narrative to an alternative one. Even the skeptical have within them this possibility. Even students who are difficult to like or understand have another side to them that can be invited out. We have faith too that a community where conflict is rife can be transformed by consistent commitment. Difficult relational contexts can be turned around using approaches that are inclusive, are respectful, and actually address problems rather than simply shifting them somewhere else.

We have primarily been addressing school leaders and school counselors/psychologists in this book. Our premise has been that these two groups need to work together to manage the processing of conflict within a school. The role of the school administrator must be tilted toward the design of systems and processes and the assigning of others to do specific tasks, but there will be occasions when she or he becomes involved in the practice of conflict resolution, too. The school counselor or psychologist has been addressed in this book more in relation to the detail of practice, but he or she should also be involved, with the school leader, in the overall design of a system of conflict management. We have envisaged a partnership that intentionally works to create relational contexts in which learning can take place. A school needs to be a learning organization itself, committed to growing new practices that go perhaps far beyond what we have articulated here.

Focusing on re-storying relationships is not a trendy gimmick for improving student test results, but rather a means of sustaining organizational growth. When teachers are instructed in a "top-down" way to use restorative practices by school authorities without adequate consultation, preparation, and training, the practices are unlikely to be sustained for long. People become disillusioned and easily slip back to punitive ways of managing students.

The comprehensive shift in the approach to school relationships we are advocating needs careful planning and a clear mandate for change from the senior leadership team. They need to be committed to the ways of speaking and relating we have consistently outlined throughout this book.

They should seek out training opportunities and then include their teaching and counseling staff in onsite training. That way, all teachers can begin to think relationally and conduct their classes along consistent lines. While it is best if all teachers treat students in a consistent way, we accept that there will be some who resist the strategies we have suggested and continue to use punitive measures to motivate students in their class. Through consistently seeing students behaving in positive ways, in noticing a reduction in violence and bullying in the school, in classroom evaluations revealing that most students are happy at school, we would hope that there will be an acceptance that the direction the school is moving is the right one. Where teachers have become demoralized and estranged from their students, the principal's or counselor's efforts to build relationships and to model a relational way of working can have a profound effect on the overall climate of the school.

However, in the absence of a schoolwide commitment to restorative practices or relational conflict resolution, individuals can begin their own private revolution and start to experiment with these ideas and to effect change slowly from within the organization.

CHOOSING THE RIGHT APPROACH

In order for what we have outlined to be effective, it is necessary to choose the right approach for the right situation. Sometimes this might mean choosing not just one approach but a combination of several. For example, a situation might call for an undercover anti-bullying team and counseling for the victim of bullying. Or a class conflict might call for a circle conversation and a guidance lesson on sexual harassment. Or a peer mediation might be followed up with referral to a "facing up to violence" group. The selection of which approach or combination of approaches to use has a number of choice points to consider. Sometimes the choice has much to do with the size of the problem and how widely its effects have spread, and a sole focus on the protagonists in the conflict story might not be enough. Repeated instances of a similar manifestation of a problem require creative thinking about what needs to be done systemically to address it.

The following subsections specify questions that can be used to determine which process is best in a particular circumstance.

Is the Conflict Between Two Individuals, or Does It Involve Larger Groups of Students?

The usual retributive approach is to assume that you can address a problem by isolating one or two individuals as the cause of it. Conflicts, however, are messy relational phenomena that have tentacle-like effects that spread through a community. Tracing these effects is perhaps more important than tracing the cause. Using Deleuze and Guattari's (1987) metaphor, they are often like a rhizome, rather than a tree. You cannot just pull out the taproot and all will be well. Often an approach is called for that addresses what is happening in networks of relations between students, rather than just between two individuals. In this situation, a class circle time may be called for or some form of restorative practice or an undercover anti-bullying team.

On the other hand, sometimes economy of action dictates the addressing of relationship stories that are at work between two individuals. Here mediation may be appropriate and may be undertaken by a peer mediator or by a counselor or psychologist. Sometimes, too, school leaders are skilled at mediation and can facilitate such conflict resolution, especially when a teacher is involved. If, however, one party to the dispute is not willing to participate in a mediation process, then the fallback position is to use conflict coaching. Useful mediation can also be facilitated, for example, when a brawl has broken out on the school grounds between two groups of students who are split along racial or ethnic lines.

Has a Disciplinary Offense Been Committed or Not?

If no significant rule has been breached, then mediation may be appropriate. If a disciplinary breach has taken place, then there needs to be a clear choice between punishment and holding students accountable through restorative practices. Different processes should not be used at the same time, or they can contaminate each other.

Restorative practices should be focused, too, on repairing harm, rather than as a sneaky way of imposing punishments. They do not work if administrators enter a conference with a fixed idea, decided in advance, of what the offender needs to do.

Restorative practices do require a degree of goodwill and participation. They are designed to maximize this, but there is no guarantee that it will always be present. If it is not, then a school may need to move to another approach, such as imposing punishment.

For restorative practices to be effective in a school, there needs to be a functioning partnership between school leaders and whoever will be designated to carry out the function of facilitating a restorative conference or conversation.

Is the Conflict Contained Within One Class, or Does It Cut Across Classes or Age Groups?

If groups of students are involved in a conflict, then it is important to establish the community within which they have membership. If it is within one class, then some inquiry should be made into whether it is happening across different subject areas. Perhaps the use of a circle conversation is indicated if the conflict is contained within the relationships of one class group.

If, on the other hand, the conflict cuts across age groups or class group-ings, then either a group mediation is called for or a guidance lesson might be designed to address a pattern of interactions that are taking place.

Is One Person Being Bullied by a Group of People, or Is It a Mutual Antagonism?

Conflict develops as a result of different desires and value systems. Often one person's perspective is as good as another's. This is what Michel Foucault (2000) referred to as ordinary power relations. Mediation can be used in situations like this to good effect. But domination is another mat-ter. Domination is where ordinary power relations get frozen into a pattern of one-way flow. It happens in families where a husband or male partner may use domestic violence and other methods to establish absolute power and control.

In the school, interpersonal domination is established through system-atic bullying behavior. The challenge is not just to identify the bully but to disrupt the bullying pattern of relationships, including the passive sup-port given to bullying by bystanders. We have offered the undercover anti-bullying team (described in Chapter 9) as one proven method of dealing with bullying. Bullying can also be interviewed using the "interviewing the problem" guidance lesson in Chapter 10.

Undercover teams work most successfully in situations of bullying within a class, where the students who are on the teams are in close regular contact with the victim. When bullying is across the age levels or occurs outside of the classroom environment—for example, when people are lin-ing up for food in the cafeteria or are in the library or on the playing fields—a restorative conversation may be more appropriate.

Another factor to consider is the relational composition of the class. In some classes, relationships may be dominated by a few students with a strong reputation for bullying. Where we have had concerns about the feasibility of an undercover team for a particular student but have gone ahead anyway, we have been pleasantly surprised by the willingness of even the strongest bullies to try out an anti-bullying reputation. The team gives them an opportunity to show students on the team who do not bully that they are able to act in a peaceful and supportive way.

What Level of Seriousness Has the Conflict Reached?

Some conflicts lead to serious assaults or very damaging relational aggression. Their effects are so powerful that they spread widely to include a number of people, not just those directly involved. For the victims of such assaults, the effects also cut deeply into their sense of themselves. It may often be the case that a school cannot tolerate the ongoing presence of someone who is willing to commit such assaults. But this should not always be assumed on the basis of the nature of the offense. The context of the offense and the degree of willingness on the part of the offending student to take responsibility for setting things right are important considerations in determining the best course of action. The action taken needs to match the seriousness of the offense and to promise a coefficient of change that makes the effort worth pursuing. A restorative conference (Chapter 6) requires effort to set up and so should not be used, unless it is fully justified. A full restorative conference must be carefully planned and may take considerable time in preparation. Some of the administration can be reduced through a standard letter inviting participants to a conference, but there is no substitute for a personal invitation. Careful thought must go into choosing the right venue, the provision of refreshments, and the recording of the conference outcomes. Because of the scale of the full restorative conference, it is most likely to affect the most people. In situations where a number of families are involved, and the violence has been extreme or there are issues beyond the classroom, a conference will have the biggest impact, especially over the longest term.

At lower levels of seriousness, a restorative conversation or undercover anti-bullying team may suffice. Or a circle conversation may be appropriate. If these are not successful, then it is necessary to slide up the scale.

Whatever the level of seriousness, the needs of the victim deserve attention. Counselors and psychologists have a special role to play in this regard. They should be willing to meet with a victim of an offense and debrief the effects of any violation that has taken place. The aim of such debriefing should be to connect the victim with his or her own resourcefulness and agency, as outlined in Chapter 3, rather than to identify pathology or invite any form of re-traumatization. If the effects of a traumatic experience require more counseling help than a school counselor or psychologist is available to provide, then it will be important to refer out.

Is One Person Caught Up in a Pattern of Problem Behavior Over a Period of Time?

We have stressed the idea that the person is not the problem in this book. But sometimes a conflict can be fueled by the way in which a problem dogs a particular individual on a regular basis or appears to take up residency in the person. Some people get into habits of fighting, or enter into a committed relationship with bullying, or repeatedly give in to the temptations of a bad temper.

In these circumstances, an interpersonal intervention such as a mediation or a restorative conversation or an undercover anti-bullying team may not be enough. Counseling is again indicated, and it may emerge in the plan to set things right in a restorative conversation or as part of an agreement in mediation. The counseling may be individual, or a commitment to participate in a "facing up to violence" group may be sought.

Has Damage Been Done That Needs to Be Addressed?

Conflict frequently produces situations in which people say things against their better judgment, which they later regret. Double listening helps us hear the desire for something better that is implicit in both the regret and the better judgment. But it also needs to be acknowledged that actions have effects and that these effects can be damaging to other people and to relationships between people. In conflict, trust can be one of the first things to fly out the window and, while the window is open, fear and anxiety may slip quietly in. Not all of the damage done in conflict is reversible, but often much of it is. Relational healing takes time, and people must not be rushed into it. But people often exhibit amazing goodwill, even in the face of substantial relational damage.

Restorative practices are designed to focus on putting things right when damage has been done. Other processes, such as conflict coaching, group counseling, and guidance lessons, can help create the ethical context for the taking of responsibility, but nothing can replace the effect of fronting up to the other (for both victims and offenders). The undercover antibullying team also creates an opportunity for bullies to put right relational damage while still saving face.

Are There a Number of Individuals Struggling With the Same Kind of Problem?

If repeated violence is shown by more than about four students, then a "facing up to violence" group might be indicated as the most economical use of professional time. Conflict coaching can also be offered in a group format when a small group of like-minded students can be identified. Likewise, it makes more sense to use a circle conversation or a group guidance lesson than to offer individual counseling on the same issue to a series of individuals in a class.

What Method of Dealing With the Problem Will Produce the Greatest Effect in the Shortest Time?

The decision about which process to use is largely pragmatic, rather than theory- or principle-driven. Conflict resolution has to contain a strong element of pragmatism in order to deliver benefits. The choice of approach is, therefore, driven by calculating the biggest effect for the most economical outlay of energy. Increasing the range of choices from which to decide leads to greater success in making this decision. Schools can also extend beyond the range we have laid out here. But sometimes the choice of action can be too economical and not address sufficiently what has happened. It is possible to multiply the effectiveness of any one method by using two or more strategies in combination. For example, a situation might demand both conflict coaching and a restorative conversation; or a circle conversation and a guidance lesson; or a restorative conference followed by counseling; or group counseling and mediation.

WHAT KINDS OF TRAINING ARE REQUIRED FOR THESE TASKS?

In order for a school to embrace the ideas in this book, leadership must come from those who have the necessary influence. Ideally, the school principal must be supportive of those on the staff who are enthusiastic about pursuing restorative approaches to relationships and be prepared to encourage the process of transformative change. Some schools go as far as adopting restorative principles as central to all school relationships. In one school, at the start of the day, the principal often reminds staff of the restorative principles the school has adopted and encourages them to use restorative conversations throughout the day. This school is continually training staff, and even the most resistant teachers are gradually realizing the benefits of a nonpunitive learning environment.

Where school staff have been directed from the top to use restorative practices without adequate consultation, preparation, and training, these practices are unlikely to be sustained in the long term. Staff become disillusioned and easily slip back to punitive ways of managing students.

On the other hand, change has to start somewhere. As suggested above, it is possible for individual teachers, counselors, and administrators to begin introducing experiments with these ideas. Students will benefit, and this will have an effect on the organization. For example, counselors can begin to use undercover teams slowly and without fanfare, and teachers can use circle conversations and restorative conversations when there is trouble. Students trained in peer mediation and peer mentoring can model the kind of relationships they prefer.

WHO MAKES THESE DECISIONS? WHO NEEDS TO BE CONSULTED?

Referrals for conflict resolution or counseling come from many sources. Students may bring a friend they are worried about, or teachers may refer students for any of the approaches in this book. Parents may phone the school with concerns about the relationships their child is experiencing, and there are cases where the school principal sets disciplinary action in motion and afterward calls for other interventions to restore relationships.

The classroom teacher can be trained to use restorative conversations, not only as an immediate response to a situation of conflict but also as a customary way of relating to her students. Such a teacher will see the relationships in her class as the very fabric of learning and will be vigilant in noticing how her students speak to her and to each other. She will model the kinds of beliefs we have outlined and will be conscious of the performative power of speech patterns in the class. Refusing to attribute to her students a label that totalizes them and speaking of conflict and trouble as if it is outside of them provides students with a way of addressing their "growing pains" with respect and real hope. She will accept that teenagers make mistakes and will focus on "putting it right." She will set clear standards of behavior from the start but will balance justice with mercy when relationship difficulties arise.

CONCLUDING REMARKS

Everybody can use the ideas in this book to conduct conversations with and about students in a way that is respectful and not demeaning. We can all refuse to buy in to discourses of homophobia and racism and can speak respectfully of individual differences. Parent Nights can be structured in such a way that students are not talked about in a dismissive way, and students can be encouraged to attend alongside their parents.

Some might object that it is not the role of schools to teach conflict resolution and that schools should concentrate on teaching reading and mathematics. To do otherwise is to conduct "experiments in social engineering." This represents a narrow, technicist view of schooling that has little to do with the noble ideals of education. Some parents and even teachers argue that students should not be taught "how to behave" but should learn this at home and be expected to already have respect for teachers and other students. This latter perspective is naïve and unsound in terms of developmental theory, and it fails to recognize that a school is a complex community.

Unfortunately, one of the effects of intensified testing regimes that concentrate school attention on a narrow range of academic outcomes is that a vision of education that is about producing citizens capable of participation in a democracy is too easily lost. One thing democracy requires is that citizens who share decision-making power must learn to work with each other and overcome the divisive power of differences. Handling such differences with respect for others is central to what education is about. That does not mean that we should set tests on conflict resolution. It means that we should take it seriously as part of the hidden curriculum that students learn by living it. Those whose job it is to think about the kind of community a school will be and about the relationships fostered within it should pay attention to the kind of climate created by the school's hidden curriculum. If they foster a climate in which the strongest always win or the loudest shout down the quietest (both teachers and students), then they are implicitly creating a world in which such values rule. But they should be clear that this is not the path that democracy walks.

It is also important that a school not be conceptualized as a factory in which "behavior" has to be "managed." To treat people as objectified commodities who are not accorded agency in their own lives is disrespectful. What we are talking about throughout our book should not, therefore, be seen as an add-on to an approach to "behavior management." It is more important than that and less objectifying. It is founded on assumptions about the importance of creating contexts for learning to practice respect. It is about according a voice to students and teachers and listening to their relational concerns. It assumes that doing so is central to what education is about. When it happens, schools start to provide the best possible arena for learning to occur.

QUESTIONS FOR REFLECTION

1. What are the most important ideas that you will take away from this book?

2. What is the best starting place for implementing these ideas in your own context?

3. Who are the allies you will work with to implement these ideas?

4. What existing practices in your school can fit well with these ideas?

QUESTIONS FOR RESEARCH

1. How could ongoing evaluation be built into the implementation of these ideas?

2. What data exist at the moment to indicate the need for introducing some of these ideas?

3. How might data be collected about the specific effects of these approaches from those most directly involved?

4. What would be the most responsive indicators of the effects of the comprehensive approach to conflict resolution in your school?

5. How might you collect a series of stories that serve as compelling illustrations of these ideas in practice?

6. How might differences in overall school climate be measured?

References

American Psychological Association Zero Tolerance Task Force. (2008). Are zero tolerance policies effective in the schools? An evidentiary review and recommendations. *American Psychologist, 63*(9), 852–862.

Argyris, C., & Schön, D. (1974). *Theory in practice: Increasing professional effectiveness.* San Francisco: Jossey-Bass.

Baruch Bush, R. A., & Folger, J. (1994). *The promise of mediation: Responding to conflict through empowerment and recognition.* San Francisco: Jossey-Bass.

Bateson, G. (1972). *Steps to an ecology of mind: Collected essays in anthropology, psychiatry, evolution, and epistemology.* Chicago: University of Chicago Press.

Besley, A. C. (2002). *Counseling youth: Foucault, power, and the ethics of subjectivity.* Westport, CT: Praeger.

Boal, A. (2002). *Games for actors and non-actors* (2nd ed.; A. Jackson, Trans.). London: Routledge.

Bourdieu, P., & Passeron, J.-C. (1977). *Reproduction in education, society and culture* (R. Nice, Trans.). London: Sage.

Braithwaite, J. (1989). *Crime, shame, and reintegration.* New York: Cambridge University Press.

Brinkert, R. (2006). Conflict coaching: Advancing the conflict resolution field by developing an individual disputant process. *Conflict Resolution Quarterly, 23*(4), 517–528.

Cobb, S. (1994). A narrative perspective on mediation. In J. P. Folger & T. S. Jones (Eds.), *New directions in mediation: Communication research and perspectives* (pp. 48–66). Thousand Oaks, CA: Sage.

Corey, M., Corey, G., & Corey, C. (2010). *Groups: Process and practice* (8th ed.). Pacific Grove, CA: Brooks/Cole.

Crick, N. R. (1995). Relational aggression: The role of intent attributions, feelings of distress, and provocation type. *Development and Psychopathology, 7,* 313–322.

Cronin-Lampe, K., & Cronin-Lampe, R. (2010). Developing a restorative school culture: The blending of a personal and professional "pilgrimage." *Explorations: An E-Journal of Narrative Practice, 1,* 14–33.

Dandurand, Y., & Griffiths, C. T. (2006). *Handbook on restorative justice programmes.* Vienna, Austria: United Nations Office on Drugs and Crime. Available at http://www.unodc.org/pdf/criminal_justice/06-56290_Ebook.pdf

Deleuze, G. (1988). *Foucault* (S. Hand, Trans.). Minneapolis: University of Minnesota Press.

Deleuze, G., & Guattari, F. (1987). *A thousand plateaus: Capitalism and schizophrenia* (B. Massumi, Trans). Minneapolis: University of Minnesota Press.

Deleuze, G., & Parnet, C. (2002). *Dialogues II* (H. Tomlinson & B. Habberjam, Trans.). New York: Columbia University Press.

Denborough, D. (2006). A framework for receiving and documenting testimonies of trauma. In D. Denborough (Ed.), *Trauma: Narrative responses to traumatic experience* (pp. 115–132), Adelaide, Australia: Dulwich Centre Publications.

Derrida, J. (1976). *Of grammatology* (G. C. Spivak, Trans.). Baltimore: Johns Hopkins University Press.

Drewery, W. (2004). Conferencing in schools: Punishment, restorative justice, and the productive importance of the process of conversation. *Journal of Community Applied Social Psychology, 14,* 332–344.

Epston, D. (2008). *Down under and up over.* Warrington, UK: AFT Publishing.

Fisher, R., & Ury, W. (1981). *Getting to yes: Negotiating agreement without giving in.* London: Penguin.

Foucault, M. (1982). Afterword: The subject and power. In H. Dreyfus & P. Rabinow (Eds.), *Michel Foucault: Beyond structuralism and hermeneutics* (pp. 199–226). Brighton, UK: Harvester Press.

Foucault, M. (2000). *Power: Essential works of Foucault, 1954–1984* (Vol. 3; J. Faubion, Ed.; R. Hurley, Trans.). New York: New Press.

Freeman, J., Epston, D., & Lobovits, D. (1997). *Playful approaches to serious problems: Narrative therapy with children and their families.* New York: Norton.

Freire, P. (1970). *Pedagogy of the oppressed.* New York: Continuum.

Gergen, K. J. (1992). *The saturated self: Dilemmas of identity in contemporary life.* New York: Basic Books.

Gergen, K. J. (1994). *Realities and relationships: Soundings in social construction.* Cambridge, MA: Harvard University Press.

Gibbs, J., & Ushijima, T. (2008). *Engaging all by creating high school learning communities.* Windsor, CA: Centersource Systems.

Gillard, J. (2010, April 10). *Address to the National Centre Against Bullying Conference,* Melbourne, Australia. Available at http://www.ncab.org.au/ConferenceInfo/

Goldstein, S. E., Young, A., & Boyd, C. (2008). Relational aggression at school: Associations with school safety and social climate. *Journal of Youth and Adolescence, 37,* 641–654.

Holder, E. (2009, October 7). *Attorney General Eric Holder speaks at news conference on youth and school violence, City Hall, Chicago.* U.S. Justice Department. Available at http://justice.gov/ag/speeches/2009/ag-speech-091007.html

Hubbard, B. (2004). *The "no-blame" bullying response approach: A restorative practice contender?* Doctoral thesis, Massey University, Auckland, New Zealand.

Jenkins, A. (1990). *Invitations to responsibility: The therapeutic engagement of men who are violent and abusive.* Adelaide, Australia: Dulwich Centre Publications.

Jones, T., & Brinkert, R. (2008). *Conflict coaching: Conflict management strategies and skills for the individual.* Thousand Oaks, CA: Sage.

Kracke, K., & Hahn, H. (2008). The nature and extent of childhood exposure to violence: What we know, why we don't know more, and why it matters. *Journal of Emotional Abuse, 8*(1/2), 29–49.

Kruk, E. (Ed.). (1997). *Mediation and conflict resolution in social work and the human services.* Chicago: Nelson-Hall.

Lindemann Nelson, H. (2001). *Damaged identities, narrative repair.* London: Cornell University Press.

McKenzie, W. (2010). Ideas and questions for critical incident work. *Explorations: An E-Journal of Narrative Practice, 1*, 34–42.

McLaren, P. (2005). Critical pedagogy and the social construction of knowledge. In E. R. Brown & K. J. Saltman (Eds.), *The critical middle school reader* (pp. 409–418). New York: Routledge.

Mirrlees-Black, C., & Byron, C. (1999). *Domestic violence: Findings from the MCS Self-Completion Questionnaire.* London: Home Office Research, Development and Statistics Directorate. Available at http://webarchive.nationalarchives .gov.uk/20110220105210/http://rds.homeoffice.gov.uk/rds/pdfs/r86.pdf

Moore, C. (1996). *The mediation process: Practical strategies for resolving conflict.* San Francisco: Jossey-Bass.

Mosley, J., & Tew, M. (1999). *Quality circle time in the secondary school: A handbook of good practice.* London: David Fulton.

Myerhoff, B. (1982). Life history among the elderly: Performance, visibility, and remembering. In J. Ruby (Ed.), *A crack in the mirror: Reflexive perspectives in anthropology* (pp. 99–117). Philadelphia: University of Pennsylvania Press.

Noddings, N. (2002). *Educating moral people: A caring alternative to character education.* New York: Teachers College Press.

Olweus, D. (1993). *Bullying at school: What we know and what we can do.* Oxford, UK: Blackwell.

Pence, E., & Paymar, M. (1993). *Education groups for men who batter: The Duluth model.* New York: Springer.

Prinstein, M. J., Boerger, J., & Vernberg, E. M. (2001). Overt and relational aggression in adolescents: Social-psychological adjustment of aggressors and victims. *Journal of Clinical Child Psychology, 30*(4), 479–491.

Restorative Practices Development Team. (2004). *Restorative practices in schools: A resource.* Hamilton, New Zealand: School of Education, University of Waikato.

Robinson, G., & Maines, B. (1997). *Crying for help: The no-blame approach to bullying.* Bristol, UK: Lame Duck Publishing.

Roth, S., & Epston, D. (1996). Consulting the problem about the problematic relationship: An exercise for experiencing a relationship with an externalized problem. In M. Hoyt (Ed.), *Constructive therapies* (Vol. 2, pp. 148–162). New York: Guilford.

Slowikowski, J. (2009). *National Survey of Children's Exposure to Violence.* Washington, DC: U.S. Department of Justice. Available at http://ojjdp.ncjrs.org/Publications/

Solomon, B. (2006). Traditional and right-informed talk about violence: High school educators' discursive production of school violence. *Youth and Society, 37*(3), 251–286.

Stuart, B. (1997). Sentencing circles: Making "real differences." In J. MacFarlane (Ed.), *Rethinking disputes: The mediation alternative* (pp. 201–232). London: Cavendish.

Tjaden, P., & Thoennes, N. (2000). *Full report of the Prevalence, Incidence, and Consequences of Violence Against Women Series.* Washington DC: National Institute of Justice and the Centers for Disease Control and Prevention. Available at http://www.ncjrs.gov/txtfiles1/nij/183781.txt

Underwood, M. K. (2003). *Social aggression among girls.* New York: Guilford Press.

U.S. Department of Education, Institute of Education Sciences. (2007). *School Survey on Crime and Safety.* Available at http://nces.ed.gov/surveys/ssocs/ tables/scs_2007_tab_14.asp

Vygotsky, L. (1978). *Mind in society: The development of higher psychological processes.* Cambridge, MA: Harvard University Press.

Vygotsky, L. (1986). *Thought and language.* Cambridge: MIT Press.

White, M. (1989, Summer). The externalizing of the problem and the re-authoring of lives and relationships. *Dulwich Centre Newsletter* [Special edition], 3–21.

White, M. (2006). Working with people who are suffering the effects of multiple trauma: A narrative perspective. In D. Denborough (Ed.), *Trauma: Narrative responses to traumatic experience* (pp. 25–86). Adelaide, Australia: Dulwich Centre Publications.

White, M. (2007). *Maps of narrative practice.* New York: Norton.

White, M., & Epston, D. (1990). *Narrative means to therapeutic ends.* New York: Norton.

Williams, M. (2010). Undercover teams: Redefining reputations and transforming bullying relationships in the school community. *Explorations: An E-Journal of Narrative Practice, 1,* 4–13.

Williams, M., & Winslade, J. (2008). Using "undercover teams" to re-story bullying relationships. *Journal of Systemic Therapies, 27*(1), 1–15.

Williams, M., & Winslade, J. (2010). Co-authoring new relationships in schools through narrative mediation. *New Zealand Journal of Counselling, 30*(2), 62–72. http://www.nzac.org.nz/nzjc.html.

Winslade, J. (2005). Utilising discursive positioning in counseling. *British Journal for Guidance and Counselling, 33*(3), 351–364.

Winslade, J. (2009). Tracing lines of flight: Implications of the work of Gilles Deleuze for narrative practice. *Family Process, 48*(3), 332–346.

Winslade, J., & Monk, G. (2000). *Narrative mediation: A new approach to dispute resolution.* San Francisco: Jossey-Bass.

Winslade, J., & Monk, G. (2007). *Narrative counseling in schools: Powerful and brief.* Thousand Oaks, CA: Corwin.

Winslade, J., & Monk, G. (2008). *Practicing narrative mediation: Loosening the grip of conflict.* San Francisco: Jossey-Bass.

Winslade, J., Monk, G., & Cotter, A. (1998). A narrative approach to the practice of mediation. *Negotiation Journal, 14*(1), 21–42.

Zehr, H. (1990). *Changing lenses.* Scottdale, PA: Herald Press.

Zehr, H. (2002). *The little book of restorative justice.* Intercourse, PA: Goodbooks.

Index

CORWIN
A SAGE Company

The Corwin logo—a raven striding across an open book—represents the union of courage and learning. Corwin is committed to improving education for all learners by publishing books and other professional development resources for those serving the field of PreK–12 education. By providing practical, hands-on materials, Corwin continues to carry out the promise of its motto: **"Helping Educators Do Their Work Better."**